CRISIS OF MORAL AUTHORITY

CRISIS OF MORAL AUTHORITY

Don Cupitt

SCM PRESS LTD

334 01958 3

First published 1972
Reissued 1985
by SCM Press Ltd
26–30 Tottenham Road, London N1

Printed in Great Britain by
Richard Clay (The Chaucer Press) Ltd,
Bungay, Suffolk

CONTENTS

PREFACE TO THE SECOND EDITION

THIS BOOK was first written in 1970, delivered as a course of Stanton Lectures at Cambridge in 1971, and published in 1972. The publisher, Cecil Northcott, had high hopes for it. There was an American edition, and even a Dutch translation. Sadly, the book never recovered from receiving favourable reviews; but now that nothing of mine is in any great danger on that score, I hope it may win a new readership.

Incidentally, that reminds me that a friend published in 1978 a perfectly sound work on christology. The reviewers gave it the kiss of death by welcoming it rapturously and declaring that if only it had appeared a year or two earlier all that sensationalist nonsense about *The Myth of God Incarnate* would never have happened. Naturally, everyone concluded that the book was a tranquillizer, so safe and boring that there was no need to read it, and even less to lay out good money for it.

My starting point in these chapters was straightforward enough. Many, perhaps most, of the great critics of Christianity have rejected it chiefly on moral grounds. Yet, because they have tended to suffer from an entrenched sense of their own moral superiority, Christians have never really taken this fact seriously enough, and so have failed fully to understand one very important factor in the modern world's rejection of faith. The idea was therefore to write a series of studies of the principal moral criticisms of Christianity, with the aim of evaluating them and discovering just how strong they are and what should be done about them.

In the original introduction I summarized the conclusions as follows: The harsh old anthropomorphic story-theology must go (Chapter 1). Much in the ascetical tradition is simply morbid (2). It is possible, though difficult, for the equality of the sexes to be realized within Christianity (3). A more genuinely liberal theology may be able to renounce physical and, still more important, psychological terrorism (4, 5), but only if the old authoritarian imagery is discarded (6), imagery which suggests that the Church, in its heart of hearts, would like to take us back into the cruel past. Christianity's alliance with the state led it to make a mistaken claim that it could underwrite or validate moral principles; in reality it *crowns* them (7). Theology must abandon the notion of a single orthodox faith, and there must be higher standards of honesty in Church life (8).

In that summary the main item which is obscure and questionable is the sentence about Chapter 7. As I now see things, I would put the point this way: in religion we symbolize, celebrate, enact and make effective our values, but we should not look to religious thought to *justify* our values.

Otherwise, the summary may stand. It shows that from the outset I must have been inclined to think that there is a good deal of weight in these moral criticisms, and that this is a serious problem.

The problem is serious *in the philosophy of religion*. If Christianity is a body of metaphysical facts from which we deduce appropriate patterns of behaviour for ourselves, then it is not clear how mere human objections to the morality that results can do anything to cast doubt on the metaphysical facts. And if so, then surely moral criticisms of Christianity are not to be taken seriously. To put it brutally, you may think Hell immoral, but there may be a Hell just the same. Accordingly, instead of questioning God's justice, you would be more prudently occupied in speedily bringing your own notions of justice into line with God's. The metaphysical facts are what they are, regardless of whether you like them or not. You should not carp about them; you should adjust yourself to them.

So it may be said. So it *should* be said, if we were still genuine theological realists. But we cannot in fact be realists, for we all of us treat a serious moral objection to a dogma as a weighty reason for doubting its *truth*. This in turn implies that our real view of religious truth must be ethical. In our hearts we know that a religion is a moral guidance-system, a whole way of life communicated to us by symbols and rituals. A serious moral objection to it is therefore a serious challenge to its ethical authority in our lives, and it is not feasible to reply to such an

8

objection by retorting that the metaphysical facts are what they are, like it or not. It is not feasible because we ourselves would not accept such a retort. Suppose we criticize the cruel punishments inflicted in modern Iran: would we accept the reply that God has ordered them and approves them?

Thus the implications of this book are anti-realist, even though the book's author refuses to grasp the point; which is why on re-reading it I laughed aloud. The straitlaced early Cupitt is so obviously struggling to prevent the later Cupitt from bursting out, especially on pp. 11–15 and in Chapter 6. Here, as so often in my early books, I zealously attack some distinguished figure for holding an opinion that I am in fact myself already well on the way to adopting.

Notice, then, what is said in the passages cited about the 'moral-projection' view of God and about Hegel's critique of objective theism. Notice, too, an unresolved conflict in my attitude to liberal theology, for pp. 98–105 contain an argument in favour of it (under the name of one-city theology), whereas the criticism on pp. 134f. of merely "supplementary" theologies is implicitly anti-liberal. It was not until the end of the seventies that I fully realized that liberal theologies are always very realist, and that they therefore represent the very antithesis of my own outlook. I have over the years gained so much from the friendship and support of various liberals that it was not easy to accept that I could only ever make my own position clear by opposing it to theirs.

Another feature of this book that deserves a brief comment is its use of the purgative way. As an undergraduate I had studied the History and Philosophy of Science and had been introduced by Russ Hanson (N. R. Hanson) to K. R. Popper. I took in the idea that natural science owes its vitality not to its possession of any body of assured truths but to the zeal with which it continually detects and expels errors from itself. Truth in science depends upon the continual cultivation of the modern intellectual virtues: doubt, scepticism, self-criticism.

Those were the days of positivism and the verification principle, a time when theology was under sharp attack. My idea was that theology might follow natural science by giving up the idea that it is in possession of any fixed deposit of truths, and

instead becoming consistently self-critical, revisionist and iconoclastic. So I brought together the Negative Way in theology,
and the Purgative Way in spirituality. Truth would lie, not in
any fixed positions, but in the direction of movement given by
the lengthy trail of broken images and abandoned illusions.

That was the idea; and this book in effect applies it to ethics.
To promote your ethic, attack its weakest points. Truth, in
theology and in ethics, is that which will stand forth after the
last illusion has been unmasked, after the last error has been
exposed. We can witness to it only indirectly, by our iconoclastic
zeal.

Naturally there was a risk that people would see what I was
doing as being "negative" and subversive. There was also a risk
that I myself would not realize to what position the method
must eventually lead me. In 1972, when this book appeared, I
certainly had no idea of where I would have to go, and the
critics were still disposed to give me the benefit of the doubt.
Hence all those dim, charitable reviews.

All these preliminary things being now said, there is not much
in the book that I would wish to change. The position of women
is better now than it was when I wrote, not least in the universities, but I leave Chapter 3 unaltered because in its day it was
fairly original. The obligation to be disingenuous, forced upon
bishops even more than upon theologians, continues to be a very
painful problem (pp. 145ff.). I cheer myself up by reporting
that the *Catholic Dictionary of Theology* maintained its form after
beginning so well – as is noted on page 33 – with "Abandonment to Casuistry". Volume Two was robustly titled, "Cate-
chism to Heaven", and then a post-Vatican II conversion was
signalled by "Hegel to Paradise".

In literary style this early work is quite bright and cheerful,
but my use of the colon, and often even of the comma, is beyond
excuse or correction. I leave it almost unchanged, an awful
warning. All biblical quotations are taken from the Revised
Standard Version.

Don Cupitt

1

THE DRAMA OF REDEMPTION
AND THE CHARACTER OF GOD

MORAL CRITICISM of religion has been going on for a long time, and is of many kinds. Sometimes it is *internal*, as when a prophet like Hosea contrasts the corrupt state of contemporary religion with its supposed earlier innocence and sincerity; and sometimes it is *external*, as when Epicurus and Lucretius argue that the social institution which is called religion is simply designed to terrorize people to no very creditable purpose.[1] When one is criticizing religion one may point out that the behaviour of religious people and institutions is at variance with their own professed ideals, or one may attack the ideals themselves.

This latter sort of criticism of religion is particularly interesting. What right have men to call the gods to account? If our moral notions are derived from religion, what right do we have to use them to attack the source from which we got them? Alternatively, if we *have* moral knowledge quite independent of religious authority, and use it to criticize religion, we seem to be well on the way to making of our religion nothing more than a projection of our own moral ideal. Religion loses any life of its own. Kant made himself a religion of this kind,[2] and so prepared the way for the sceptical and critical reductions of religion which followed in the next century.

Here is an awkward dilemma. How do we think of God? Do we, like Job, think of him as a terrible actual being and then ask whether he is good? Or do we, like many moderns, think of him as the personification of final moral value, and then ask if he is actual?

[1] Lucretius, *De Rerum Natura*, I, 62–145.
[2] *Religion with the Limits of Reason Alone* (1793).

For Job, God was a terrible actual being with which men must come to terms willy-nilly. There was no escaping him, perhaps not even in death. God was integral to the way people responded to and described the world: atheism was not a serious possibility. You prayed God to be merciful and gracious because you knew very well that he was quite capable of being otherwise. Confronted with the facts of evil, moral and physical, men might be led, with Job, to question God's justice: but they did not doubt his existence. Gods are slippery, inscrutable beings. A god might swear everlasting support to the house of David, and then withdraw it; a god might promise to be friend of the righteous man, and then in a fit of caprice, allow him to be ruined; a god might create man, and then repent it and try to destroy him; a god might make Saul King, and then change his mind. Gods were arbitrary and high-handed; that was to be expected. But gods and men needed each other, and a shrewd man must learn how to handle his god with cunning. God must be reproached, wheedled and humoured. You must, like the Psalmist, appeal to his better nature, remind him of his professed passion for justice, recall days when he behaved better, and encourage him to think of his own reputation. Men learned to cope with God as a capable woman learns to cope with an ill-tempered husband, as a child learns to cope with its father, or as a man learns to domesticate a wild animal. In those days you worshipped God because you had better, to keep him sweet-tempered. Worshipping god was a highly-developed social skill. It needed elaborate techniques to manage someone so jealous, so inquisitive, so liable to dangerous fits of rage, yet so loving when in the right frame of mind.[1]

But the modern man approaches the question of God in a quite different way. Since the rise of natural and historical sciences emancipated from theology, God is no longer integral to the ways in which we describe the scene about us. Belief in God is no longer culturally compulsory, but optional. God is seen more as a moral postulate. We think of him as perfect

[1] For attempts to convey to a modern reader the "feel" of ancient belief, see C. G. Jung, *Answer to Job* (1952; ET 1954) and C. S. Lewis, *Till we have Faces* (1956) —two very odd books.

goodness and love, the moral ideal embodied, and then ask whether our experience of life is such as to lead us to suppose that God exists. So we respond to the facts of evil by doubting God's existence, rather than by assuming his existence but doubting his goodness.[1] The suggestion that there might be a god who is capricious, terrible and not good as we are good is greeted with incredulity and indignation.[2]

Much of our religious thought is affected by this change of approach. If Jesus is recorded in the Gospels as making some morally offensive statement, it has become a common reaction to suppose that he cannot have said such a thing: it is inconsistent with his character and must be a secondary addition.[3]

Here are two examples of the changeover to a "moral-projection" approach to the question of God. First, John Stuart Mill's account of his father's unbelief.[4] As has been true of most English freethinkers, "my father's rejection of all that is called religious belief, was not, as many might suppose, primarily a matter of logic and evidence; the grounds of it were moral, still more than intellectual. He found it impossible to believe that a world so full of evil was the work of an Author combining infinite power with perfect goodness and righteousness." Like Lucretius, James Mill regarded religion as socially harmful in that it diverted men from the pursuit of genuine virtues to bogus ones like faith and piety. But worst of all was the moral harm done by worshipping odious gods. The God of Christianity was the "*ne plus ultra* of wickedness", "a being who would make a Hell— who would create the human race with the infallible foreknowledge, and therefore the intention, that the great majority of them were to be consigned to horrible and everlasting torment". Now the Bible itself says that men tend to become like what they worship.[5] Surely if James Mill is right the most serious Christians ought to be the most ferocious

---

[1] Cf. Camus' saying that "the only excuse for God is that he does not exist".

[2] Cf. the response of F. D. Maurice and J. S. Mill to H. L. Mansel, of which I have written elsewhere.

[3] A Victorian example in H. Rashdall, *Conscience and Christ* (1916), pp. 183f.

[4] *Autobiography* (1873), Chapter II.

[5] E.g. Psalm 135: 18.

bigots? James Mill himself saw the difficulty. Most Christians, he conceded, are not as wicked as their professed God. What they really worship is "their own idea of excellence". They suffer a good deal by their efforts to reconcile the God of their official theology with their private ideal of perfect goodness, and so the moral tradition of Christian countries is in an unhappy jumble. Here then, in James Mill, is a suggestion that the effective deity of the modern believer is the moral ideal, and not "the objective Deity" of popular religion, who is more of a liability than an asset.

The second example is from another book published in the same year, Matthew Arnold's *Literature and Dogma* (1873). Arnold discusses the word "God". Now Arnold is an unphilosophical writer, and it is hard to be sure just what he means, but this is what he says:[1] the word "God" is not usually used as "a term of science or exact knowledge", designating a clearly-understood object. No such "science of God" is possible. Arnold detests dogmatic theology, which he thinks has quite misunderstood the Bible. Instead, he quotes Luther, who connected "Gott" with "Gutt" and defined God as "the best that man knows or can know"—that is, a projection of the moral ideal. Arnold actually uses the metaphor of *throwing-out*. "God" is a term of poetry and eloquence, a term "thrown out" at a not-fully-grasped object, a term meaning different things to different people. In the claims of morality the old Hebrews saw something *not-ourselves*, in us and around us, making its claim upon us: it became to them "adorable eminently and altogether as a power that makes for righteousness; which makes for it unchangeably and eternally, and is therefore called *the Eternal*". This notion of "the Eternal not ourselves which makes for righteousness" is not a metaphysical notion; it springs from moral experience, deeply felt, and expressed in the language of poetry.

So here in Arnold we can see a very definite change from a real but morally-dubious god to a morally-perfect but dubiously real God. In a confused way, no doubt, he highlights a very important change in the character of religious thought. And

[1] In Chapter I.

this change makes the whole subject of moral criticism of religion very complicated.

Let us set about tracing out the story, beginning with the Greeks. The Greeks told stories about their gods, and Xenophanes of Colophon criticized these stories on two counts. First, the stories are patently anthropomorphic: "The Ethiopians say that their gods are snub-nosed and black; the Thracians that theirs have light blue eyes and red hair: if they could draw as men can, horses would draw the forms of the gods like horses." In the second place, the stories are immoral: "Homer and Hesiod have attributed to the gods everything that is a shame and reproach among men, stealing and committing adultery and deceiving each other."[1] A third proposition, completing the case, is best exemplified in Plato:[2] unedifying tales about gods have a harmful moral influence. A man might justify his conduct by citing such a story as a precedent. If the business of religion is to imitate and become more like the divine,[3] then in a well-ordered state the authorities should ensure that the gods set a good example.

Christians too tell stories about God. Indeed classical Christianity was expressed in a single gigantic story, told with a specific purpose. This story[4] arose, more than anything else, as an answer to the problem of evil, a problem which is rightly supposed to be especially pressing for Christian believers.

The problem is usually set up like this. Christian believers maintain that the following three propositions are each and all true:

1. God is all-powerful.
2. God is all-benevolent.
3. There is much misery in the world.

But if any two of these propositions are true, says the critic,

[1] Frr. 169–172; in G. S. Kirk and J. E. Raven, *The Presocratic Philosophers* (1957), pp. 168f.

[2] *Republic*, II, 376E–392C; tr. F. M. Cornford (1941), pp. 65ff.

[3] *Theaetetus*, 176C.

[4] Here and throughout I use "story" in a quite general sense, which might include myth, history, or any other kind of narrative. I am interested particularly in the way stories are told to *explain* things.

the third cannot be true. Here, says a professional philosopher,[1] "we have a mathematical proof bearing on a common religious doctrine. Anyone who is confident that he frequently comes across misery in the world may conclude with equal confidence that there is no such thing as an all-powerful and all-benevolent god. And this mathematically disposes of official Christianity. . . .".

The word "mathematical" is too strong, and its repetition betrays a touch of insecurity. Mr. Robinson has overstated the case. What the Christian, like the Jew before him, did was to tell a great story: and the question is not a simple one of mathematics, but a difficult one of whether a story works. For the story is told with the design of showing that in spite of everything God is loving; he is working to overthrow evil and vindicate himself, and he will be victorious. It is described as "the plan of salvation" or "the drama of redemption", and is derived principally, but not solely, from the Bible. Some episodes in the story, but not many, are mythologized versions of historical occurrences which can be investigated by historical methods; but on the whole the story is best described as an immensely rich and detailed mythical narrative, reaching from the creation of the angels to the consummation of all things, which at certain key points incorporates historical events, and professes to supply the key to understanding the whole of history.

Briefly, the story was built in three stages. There was an Israelite historical nucleus, which came to be set in a vastly elaborated mythological frame: then a Christian historical nucleus was inserted and integrated with the inherited Jewish faith, and finally the whole was again progressively elaborated.

The Jewish historical nucleus described the historical events which had brought the nation into being, and attributed them to the agency of God. There were various elements in this tradition—the Exodus, the Covenant on Mount Sinai, the House of David, and the Temple with its cult. These elements were incorporated into a long historical narrative and elaborated mythically. The beginning of God's interest in Israel was pushed back, from Moses to Abraham, from

[1] Richard Robinson, *An Atheist's Values* (1964), p. 124.

16

Abraham to Noah, from Noah to Adam, and from Adam to the angels. When prophecies of a restoration from the Babylonian exile were fulfilled, not only was the historical nucleus extended (to describe the reconstruction of the City, its wall, its temple and its Law), but a great impetus was given to eschatological speculation. The coming of the Messiah, the general resurrection, the last battle against the forces of evil, the final division of angels and men into good and evil, and the end of all things, were described in various ways.

Into this now enormous structure the Christians inserted their early preaching (the *kerygma*). It argued that old prophecy was now fulfilled, and told its own story, of the Baptist, and of the Ministry, death, and vindication of Jesus. Then it told of the gift of the Spirit, and ended with a conclusion which combined eschatological with hortatory themes.

This new insertion into the old structure gradually demanded a thorough revision of it. Since Christianity was a religion of salvation from sin, much more emphasis had to be given to the Fall, which made salvation necessary. The entire structure was thoroughly revised to point forward to the incarnation of God in Christ, showing that it was intended from the first. The mythopoeic imagination surrounded Jesus with a mythological frame. Strange stories were told of his birth, mighty works, Resurrection and Ascension. A Christian eschatology was gradually developed, after some false starts.

The final form of the story was sealed, for the West, by Augustine, who was the first to insist that Church history down to the present time should be included in it,[1] and built into it his characteristic doctrine of the two cities. In Augustine's writings the story is told over and over again, whether in brief summary (*De Fide et Symbolo*, 393) or at full length (*De Civitate Dei*, 413–426). As the *De Catechizandis Rudibus* (about 405) makes clear, teaching someone Christianity is just expounding in full the story told in outline in the creeds. The purpose of telling the story is quite simply to awaken love for God.

According to the ancient rhetorical theory, any oration

---

[1] *The First Catechetical Instruction* (*de Cat. Rud.*), tr. and annotated by J. P. Christopher (1946), p. 5.

should begin with an *exordium* and then plunge into the *narratio*, an "exposition of things done".[1] Christian teaching, addressed to catechumens, also consisted mainly of *narration*. Everything in the narration was to be governed by the aim of showing God to be loving, and awakening love for God in the hearer. He would be smitten with awe, with fear of God's sternness, and with admiration for God's patience and contrivance: but love was the controlling thought.

Augustine's version of the story was not the only version, though it has been the most influential. Some distinguished theologians have told a story very different from his.[2] The first modern attempt at a radical break came with Schleiermacher.[3] But the influence of the classical story has certainly not been shaken off yet, even though it now seems so strange that when J. S. Bezzant outlined it he had to end by saying that "the bare recital of it has the aspect of a malicious travesty".[4] The story remains influential because of its narrative drive, its dramatic grandeur, its harshness, and its power to inspire individual and community with a sense of an unfolding destiny in which each has a part to play.[5] Students at the moment are greatly influenced by Professor John Hick's book *Evil and the God of Love* (1966), which argues for a version of the story founded on Irenaeus rather than the familiar one founded on Augustine. But the story is still basically the same story, and one ends the book having accepted many of the criticisms of Augustine's story and yet with undiminished awe at its greatness.

To return now to our argument, Christian theology has consisted very largely in an attempt to answer the problem of evil by telling this great story. No two theologians tell it identically, but the story is recognizably the same story, whether told by John of Damascus, Anselm, Aquinas, Luther, Calvin or Barth. But a story as such becomes subject to the

[1] *The First Catechetical Instruction* (*de Cat. Rud.*), tr. and annotated by J. P. Christopher (1946), p. 95, n. 9.
[2] For example, Origen, *On First Principles*, ed. G. W. Butterworth (1936).
[3] *The Christian Faith* (1821–22).
[4] *Objections to Christian Belief*, ed. A. R. Vidler (1963), p. 84.
[5] See the tribute paid recently by J. H. Plumb in *The Death of the Past* (1969), pp. 68–85.

judgement of a literary critic. He can ask, does it ring true? Do the actions of the characters make sense? Indeed, do they make *moral* sense? What kind of character does the story attribute to God?

The point of telling a story in religion is that of all literary forms the story most demands the exercise of imagination. To *follow* a story one must identify with and feel with its characters.[1] To follow the story of the Prodigal Son is in imagination to become the younger son and feel as he felt; perhaps too to become the elder brother, and the father. Where the story is a great religious myth about superhuman characters there are obvious difficulties, and at least the more cautious theologians duly protest the inadequacy of language.[2] As a story, the story must anthropomorphize. Its characters, God and Satan included, can only be understood dramatically, that is, as *dramatis personae*, by being humanized. But the story also has to show God's almighty power. It is one of Milton's difficulties that God is both a character within the story, engaged dramatically with the other characters, and also the omnipotent author of the entire story and all the characters. How can the dramatic interest of the story survive the realization that one of the characters is omnipotent? Does it not threaten to become a cat-and-mouse game?

From this source spring the principal moral difficulties of the story, and they are very acute. It is easy to accept that the terms we use to speak of God have, and cannot but have, a certain comical inadequacy about them. But it is not easy to accept that God will appear morally repellent, however the story be told: and the question at issue is whether we do indeed have to accept that proposition. To answer the problem of evil and awaken love for God a story must be told. The story is one of fall and redemption. It shows God at work, battling against evil, and it promises his final victory. It can be told in many ways, but can it be told successfully, or will God appear morally repellent, however the story be told?

[1] On following a story, see W. B. Gallie, *Philosophy and the Historical Understanding* (1964).
[2] As Augustine himself constantly does.

It can sometimes happen that one or two deeds in a man's life can persuade us that he is a good man in spite of the fact that the rest of his life gives a good deal of evidence to the contrary. Boswell tells such a story about Samuel Johnson.[1] On his way home one evening the old Doctor found a woman collapsed in the street. He picked her up and carried her home on his back. In his odd household she was nursed back to health, and Johnson "endeavoured to put her into a virtuous way of living". This touching little story, with its overtones of the Good Samaritan, may well persuade us that even if Johnson was often overbearing, ill-mannered and bad-tempered, he was after all a very good man.

Similarly, in the story of God's dealings with the human race, it might be claimed that what he showed himself to be in Jesus atones for the harsher side he shows at other points in the story. Professor Basil Mitchell once made up a story with the purpose of illustrating this claim.[2]

But the main objection to this argument is that the greatest moral difficulty in the Christian story occurs at the very points upon which the whole plot turns—the origin of evil, election, the fall, and the method of redemption.

The modern period is distinguished by the enormous popularity of fiction as a literary form. The Victorians loved a story, and they liked stories to be morally edifying. When they read a story they were accustomed to ask if the story was edifying, and to make moral judgements upon the characters in the story. Suppose then we consider the Plan of Salvation (as described by Augustine, Calvin or Jonathan Edwards) as if it were the plot of a Victorian novel. What kind of impression do we get of God, the principal character in the story? Imagine that God is the novelist, writing the history of the world. Has he made a morally edifying plot?

S. T. Coleridge put the difficulty well: a man may want to believe in Christianity, and, if he does, he is not likely to be

---

[1] It can be found by looking up the name of Mrs. Desmoulins in an indexed edition.

[2] *New Essays in Philosophical Theology*, eds. A. G. N. Flew and A. C. MacIntyre (1955), pp. 103ff.

troubled overmuch by articles of faith which are simply above his comprehension. It is only where the belief required of him jars badly with his moral feelings, contradicts his clear notions of right and wrong, and seems to be incompatible with belief in the divine goodness and justice, that he is likely to be alienated. "Such are the Doctrines", says Coleridge, "of Arbitrary Election and Reprobation; the Sentence to ever-lasting Torment by an eternal and necessitating decree; vicarious Atonement, and the necessity of the Abasement, Agony and ignominious Death of a most holy and meritorious Person, to appease the wrath of God."[1] These are turning-points in the story: it is essential that morally satisfactory accounts be given of how it has come about that all men are in need of redemption, whether all or some only shall gain it, and by what means.

Nor is it correct to say that Calvinism, or the debased form of it which in middle-class Victorian England bore the name of "Evangelicalism", must bear the reproach alone. Much the same problems are discussed in the field of Dante-criticism as in the field of Milton criticism. C. S. Lewis, in *A Preface to Paradise Lost* (1942) "decided that the beliefs used by the poem are those central to any Christian theology, except for some minor and doubtful points", and an occasional "imprudence" on the poet's part; and, on this at least, Empson agrees with him.[2]

The moral revolt against Christian orthodoxy in early Victorian England was violent. As Coleridge had foretold, the *cruces* were the doctrines of the Fall and Original Sin, of the Atonement, and of Hell. Howard R. Murphy has described the reaction against them of Francis Newman, J. A. Froude, and Mary Ann Evans (George Eliot).[3] Murphy says that these intellectuals perceived a fundamental opposition between orthodox dogma "and the meliorist ethical bias of the age".

[1] *Aids to Reflection* (1825), "Aphorisms on Spiritual Religion": Bohn edn. (1901), p. 103.

[2] See William Empson, *Milton's God* (1961, revised 1965), p. 9.

[3] "The Ethical Revolt Against Christian Orthodoxy in Early Victorian England"; *The American Historical Review*, Vol. LX, No. 4, July 1955. In these cases the reaction was wonderfully helped by two pious brothers and a father.

Christianity had always taught otherworldly salvation; but the new age held that man's life on earth could be bettered by sustained human effort. There is something in this, but it is not the whole story. More to the point is nineteenth-century "republicanism": the moral seriousness, the emphasis on the individual conscience, on liberty, on the reform of the content of the law and the way it was administered. It seemed wrong to the nineteenth century to punish a man for holding the wrong religious beliefs—but God apparently still did so. The purpose of punishment began to be seen as remedial—but God punished retributively and endlessly. Consider how the Victorians felt about the damnatory clauses in the Athanasian Creed.[1] God seemed morally archaic. He could punish the entire race for one man's sin. The traditional argument that we were seminally present in Adam's loins cut no ice with the Victorians, who made a sharp distinction between the realms of nature and of morality, as we do. A son should not be punished for his father's offence, nor should the innocent be punished in order to expiate the offence of the guilty. The Victorians thought it a moral duty to believe that no one was quite beyond redemption: they did not like the doctrine of Reprobation, and if a Broad Church clergyman questioned the doctrine of eternal punishment he might, with Maurice, be reviled by the theologians, but he was sure of the sympathy of a large public of liberal-minded laymen.

The Victorians particularly disliked the morality of the Old Testament. Tom Paine's *Age of Reason* (1793–95, 1807) was the most influential sceptical work throughout the century:[2] it last made a convert in 1939. Paine was shocked by the cruelty of the massacres in (for example) the Book of Joshua.[3] They are

[1] There is an account of the Athanasian Creed controversy in P. T. Marsh, *The Victorian Church in Decline* (1969), Chapter 2.

[2] See Susan Budd, "The Loss of Faith: Reasons for Unbelief among Members of the Secular Movement in England, 1850–1950"; *Past and Present*, No. 36, April 1967. Her final sentence is: "The loss of faith for Freethinkers was not an intellectual but a moral matter".

[3] A just verdict on Paine in Leslie Stephen, *A History of English Thought in the Eighteenth Century* (1876), Chapter 8, Part 7; and see how feeble was the *Reply to Paine* (1796) of Richard Watson. For Paine's ridicule of the Christian story, see *The Age of Reason*, Part I, Chapters IV and V.

a constant cause of complaint throughout nineteenth-century literature.[1]

Even where Christian doctrine was not morally archaic, it was sometimes depressingly crude. W. E. Gladstone was not a man given to irreverence, but he complained that "The Redemption of Man was treated . . . as a joint stock transaction between God and man with Christ as the broker. One acquired 'a saving interest in the blood of Jesus'".[2]

The early Victorians had not read Kant,[3] but like him they believed in duty for duty's sake, and they did not like the prominence given to rewards and punishments in the Christian story.

It would be wrong to suggest that the moral criticisms of the traditional Christian story are peculiar to the nineteenth century. Many of them were urged by the pagan Celsus, against whom Origen took up his pen in the third century.[4] In England, John Locke, by stressing the appeal to reason and conscience of the Christian message, had inadvertently licensed the Deists to say that in their judgement much in Christianity was, on the contrary, offensive to reason and conscience. When Tom Paine announced that he had discovered that the Old Testament, and the doctrines of Original Sin and the Atonement, were immoral, he was merely repeating to a large popular audience what the Deists had said to a small audience. But after Paine wrote it was plain that there was now a very considerable gap between divine standards of justice and human standards of justice. God's way of behaving, as pictured in the received orthodox doctrines, looked cruel and archaic, rather as the Church Courts (at least, till very recently) fell far short of the secular courts in their standards; or as the Church's mode of government, at all levels, seems

[1] Dickens and Thackeray on this subject in W. O. Chadwick, *The Victorian Church*, I (1966), pp. 528f.

[2] Cited by Noel Annan, *Leslie Stephen* (1951), p. 120; and see the note on p. 303.

[3] Coleridge read Kant, but did not like his ethics. Wordsworth's *Ode to Duty* (as its opening line betrays) borrows from Milton, not Kant. The first accurate exposition of Kant's thought came from Mansel in 1856; the first book from Edward Caird in 1877.

[4] See *Origen : Contra Celsum*, ed. and tr. H. Chadwick (1953).

today to fall short of the best standards of a secular liberal democracy. A kind of moral updating of Christianity was necessary, and so a large part of nineteenth-century theology was devoted to attempts at retelling the Christian story in such a way as to avoid the more obvious moral objections to it. This is very obvious in the German tradition which stems from F. D. E. Schleiermacher, but it can also be observed in theologians outside that great tradition, who were often men of a much more conservative cast of mind.

Take, for example, the doctrine of Original Sin. The classical Protestant doctrine saw Adam's sin as the last free act before Christ. It plunged all mankind into a state of depravity and bondage. Our sins prior to justification by Christ were necessitated, and yet, supposedly, truly sins. The corruption of our nature was congenital, and yet, supposedly, blameworthy. Adam fell, even though free and assisted by all manner of superadded graces, and this is doubtless very blameworthy. We are born fallen, deprived of these graces (though our need of them is presumably still greater than his), and yet our sins, which we have no choice but to commit, merit eternal damnation.

It is hard to see how these doctrines could be embodied in any story which would show God in a favourable light. It is hard to see how those who framed them thought they could. The nearest analogy I can think of is the old Chinese etiquette. When one Chinaman met another he would say "How is your honourable self this morning?" The other would reply, "My vile and unworthy self is very well." He might continue, "Where is your splendid palace?"; and the other would reply "My miserable hovel is on the hill over there." In a similar vein, a Japanese might say "This is my pig of a wife", and the other would reply, "Your pig of a wife is plump and fair." The idea was that politeness demanded that you should always denigrate yourself and your possessions, and grotesquely flatter the other man. Applied to God, the supreme Potentate, a similar sense of etiquette might require you to ascribe all goodness and holiness to him, all vileness and baseness to yourself. He is all-holy, you are all-sinful; he alone performs all your good deeds, you alone are to blame for all your evil deeds.

But if God is creator there is a limit to how far you can go in magnifying the creator by vilifying his creature; if God is good, it seems odd to insist that his world is entirely given over to sin. How can he be worshipped if men have nothing good to offer him, and if his government is pictured as being incompetent or unjust, or both?

Nineteenth-century theologians saw the difficulty. Schleiermacher virtually abandoned original righteousness, and the Fall as a declension from it.[1] He analysed original sin into two elements. First, he said that there is in men a natural or lower consciousness (a survival of his animal background, as F. R. Tennant[2] was later to say) upon which the consciousness of God supervenes only slowly, through long ages.[3] The persistence in us of the natural, and the reluctance with which it gives its due supremacy to the divine, is not as such blameworthy. Mankind, as a matter of fact, only evolves gradually. Secondly, there is an inherited social tradition of sin: we are born into a sinful society, which is collectively blameworthy.[4] The idea of an inherited sinful *culture* (rather than sinful *nature*) has been adopted even by so conservative a theologian as Austin Farrer:[5] "It is not our parents' loins, but our parents' lives, that enslave us."

Coleridge, too, saw very clearly the moral difficulties of a doctrine of Original Sin,[6] even as propounded by so un-Calvinistical a divine as Jeremy Taylor. Following Kant, he finds the origin of sin in the will; *my* sin must originate in *my* will: it *cannot* be "inherited". It is not too strong to say that the traditional doctrine causes Coleridge something like moral torment. The solution he reaches is that Adam is not a proper name, but the name of a genus. Adam is Everyman, every man

[1] *The Christian Faith*, §61.
[2] *The Origin of Sin* (1902).
[3] *The Christian Faith*, §67.
[4] *ibid.*, §71.
[5] E.g. *Love Almighty and Ills Unlimited*, (1962), pp. 150–160.
[6] *Aids to Faith*, Aphorism XII on Spiritual Religion; Bohn edn. (1901), pp. 172–195.

who looks into his conscience sees that he is Adam: "in respect of Original Sin *every* man is the adequate representative of *all* men."[1] Let us say no more than that, and perhaps give up story-telling: move straight from conscience to Christ. Coleridge cuts the story to the barest minimum.

Kierkegaard, another poet, layman, and strongly conservative in temperament, also feels acutely the moral objections to the doctrine of Original Sin.[2] Because of his extreme moral individualism he has great difficulty in relating the individual to the community or race. Sin cannot be a necessary stage in the evolution of consciousness—or it would not be *sin*; it cannot be an inherited necessity—or it would not be sin. Kierkegaard's solution is like Coleridge's: each individual includes the race within himself. But he was not altogether satisfied with this rather Hegelian answer, and not even his unrivalled gifts as a contortionist can enable him to reconcile the autonomy of the moral agent, the link with Adam, and the repudiation of Pelagianism.

So in modern times it has proved very difficult to reshape the earlier episodes in the story which tell of the origin and propagation of sin. But the doctrine of the Atonement presents even more serious difficulties. The first part of the story showed how evil appeared, without God being at fault. The next task is to represent dramatically the process of thought by which God works out a solution to the problem. The story has usually described an inner conflict in God between his justice and his mercy to which the Incarnation is the solution. It makes a fine drama, but there is something disagreeable in the picture of God's being torn between the principle that a heavy penalty for sin must be paid, and a principle that mercy must be shown; and something even more disagreeable in the way God uses his Son to solve his own problem.

The Victorians idealized childhood and family life. The way they created a magical literature of childhood is far removed

---

[1] *Aids to Faith*, p. 194.
[2] Especially *The Concept of Dread* (1844), Chapter I: ET by Lowrie, 1944, Second Edition, 1957. See also the discussion by L. Dupré, *Kierkegaard as Theologian* (ET 1963), pp. 49ff.

from the old assumption that children are born wicked. So too, in the 1960s, when the baptismal rite was turned into the vernacular, the Roman Catholic laity were startled to realize that their children were being exorcized. It seemed a long way from Dr. Benjamin Spock. And in the modern period the doctrine of the Atonement must be related to the way we conceive the relation of fathers to sons.

If the story is to *be* a story it must represent God as constrained by certain necessities—as being in a dilemma for which the Incarnation and death of Christ are the one and only solution. But how can God be constrained by necessities which he himself has imposed: and what of the solution? In the story, God and Christ must be pictured either as like one human person or as like two. If the story treats God and Christ as one person we have a rather absurd picture of God driving a hard bargain with himself, and punishing himself in order to appease his own wrath. Or, in a more modern idiom, a picture of a General who has bungled and goes to the front to die with his troops, by way of showing that he regrets his error. But if the story represents God and Christ as two distinct individuals, then the Son is pictured as volunteering, because *noblesse oblige*, to be the hapless victim of his own father's righteous anger. Neither picture is attractive, so how can any compromise between them be so? However the story be set up, we have the impression that, if it is going to work as a story, the story will be an ugly one.[1]

Once again, nineteenth-century theologians saw the difficulty and tried to retell the story, or virtually abandoned it.

But now we must draw the threads together. The classical story was developed as an answer to the problem of evil. As such it does not work well. The truth is that the more "objective" your theology is, the more you will suppose yourself to be in possession of a kind of literal account of God's nature and dealings with men, and the more open your belief will be to severe moral criticism. This is as true of

---

[1] See for example William Empson, *Milton's God*; and in the light of that book consider the argument of Anselm's *Cur Deus Homo* (reprinted in E. R. Fairweather, *A Scholastic Miscellany: Anselm to Ockham*, 1956).

sophisticated theology as it is of popular realistic faith. An Anselm or a Milton has almost negligible success in trying to dramatize the story in a way which will justify the ways of God to men. In fact it is the most highly developed dogmatic theologies which represent God in the most repellent light. And it will not do to say, "It's only symbolism", if the symbolism is in fact morally repellent. It is all very well to say that we can only *think* God through imperfect symbols: but how can it be our duty to be *guided in the moral life* by morally-repellent symbols?

It is because of the weakness of the old story that the complaint is so often heard that "the Churches have no answer to the problem of evil". And the weakness of the story is primarily a *moral* weakness. From Paine and Bentham to Russell and Empson, prominent unbelievers have disbelieved mainly on *moral* grounds.[1] Christian apologetic has often been ineffectual in that believers have unconsciously assumed the moral superiority of Christianity and so have been reluctant to consider these moral objections with the seriousness they deserve.

Are the immoralities the inevitable result of trying to tell an anthropomorphic story? I think so. A very clear example is the doctrine of God's aseity or self-sufficiency. Deep in religion is the idea of a condition of perfect bliss or beatitude, undisturbed and calm: a perfection and beauty simple, total, and complete. It appears in the concept of nirvana, in the self-contemplation of Aristotle's God,[2] in the prophet Ezekiel's assertion that the end of God's action is always his own glory,[3] in the everlasting rest of the saints, in the secure beatitude of the Epicurean gods. The purpose, or *a* purpose, of religion always was and always will be to lead men away from suffering, restlessness, anxiety, and contrivance, to a state of tranquil bliss. Theistic religions represent God as enjoying such a state, and inviting believers to share it.

---

[1] For Russell's unbelief see E. S. Brightman's contribution to *The Philosophy of Bertrand Russell*, ed. P. A. Schilpp (1946).

[2] *Metaphysics* Λ, 1074. (Everyman translation, 1956, pp. 345ff.)

[3] Chapter 36.

There is, I think, nothing *intrinsically* morally repugnant about such an ideal. One of Kierkegaard's most moving and beautiful discourses was that on the Unchangeableness of God and the comfort that is in that immutability.[1]

But as soon as you try to represent it anthropomorphically it at once becomes repugnant. God looks self-satisfied, indifferent, smug, complacent, callous. His impervious bliss seems hard-hearted. After the First World War, there was a good deal of questioning of the traditional doctrine of the impassibility of God.[2] But it was, I think, misguided. God had been thought too anthropomorphically.

So I conclude that the traditional expression of Christianity in the form of a drama or cosmic redemption myth was probably a mistake. For it seems that no such story can be satisfactorily told. It is unfortunate that the story still pervades the liturgy and popular teaching of the churches at a time when theologians are turning away from it.

[1] Delivered May 18, 1851; published 1855; translated by D. F. Swenson and published in several places: with *For Self-Examination* (1941); in R. Bretall's *Kierkegaard Anthology* (1946); and with a selection of *Edifying Discourses* (1958).

[2] See J. K. Mozley, *The Impassibility of God* (1926).

2

ASCETICISM

SCARCELY ANY aspect of Christianity has been the object of such widespread and constant moral repugnance as Christian asceticism. The subject is very emotionally-loaded even today. Not long ago there was an international uproar over the recruiting of Indian girls from Kerala by European religious houses of women. Even if the allegations were true, it is hard to see why there should be such a scandal unless old feelings of disgust and antipathy towards the religious life are still active. I think they are: for many people, now as much as in the last century, the religious life is a phenomenon which arouses astonishment, and pity. It may be allowed that the life suits a few people, but the thought of anyone being forced into it by poverty or parental pressure is shocking, and the suggestion that entry to it might be sought as a privilege by gifted and healthy people is scarcely credible.

These strong feelings have been compounded by ignorance. In most religions we can find ascetical regulations governing conduct whose *rationale* is hard to discover. They survive, and are zealously observed, long after the believers have forgotten their original meaning. Only with the development of modern anthropology has there been a possibility of recovering it.

A good example is the Jewish Law defining clean and unclean animals, to be found in Chapter 11 of Leviticus. Between the first century before Christ and the 1960s no known commentator gives anything like a correct explanation of this apparently bizarre list of what animals may and may not be eaten. Allegorical exegesis was popular. Parting the hoof meant discerning between good and evil, chewing the cud

30

meant ruminating wisely. For over 2000 years Jews observed the food laws while no one alive knew what they meant, so that they were constantly open to the standard criticism of sceptics, that they were superstitious, irrational, and the like; and no very good defence was available.

Yet the true explanation of the food laws is surprisingly simple.[1] They belonged to a pastoral people whose economy was based on cattle, sheep, and goats. A good herdsman would be ashamed to be reduced to living off wild game. His business was with cloven-hoofed, ruminant ungulates. If he were to take any wild game, it should preferably be other animals of the same kind. The regulations rule out various marginal cases—animals which chew, or seem to chew, the cud but do not part the hoof, and animals which part the hoof but do not chew the cud.

The second principle determining the form of the list is the belief in the order of God's creation. There are three media in which creatures move. In the air there ought to be two-legged feathered creatures with wings. On the land there ought to be four-legged beasts that walk, run, and hop. In the water there ought to be scaly creatures with fins. The proper order is birds in the air, beasts in the field, fishes in the sea. Creatures that break this order are anomalous and disagreeable and ought to be avoided. Birds of prey that behave like carnivorous mammals, water birds and flightless birds are out of order; so are flying insects, though a flying locust that can hop about properly on the ground is tolerable. Mammals that fly, burrow or crawl are wrong, especially those like the mole, which have forelimbs like hands but nevertheless obstinately crawl on their bellies, and snakes and worms which have no proper limbs at all. Fish such as eels are disagreeable, because they do not have proper fins.

So by observing the food laws the ancient Israelite was expressing his faith in the proper order of creation, his place in God's ordered world as a member of a pastoral society. The notion of holiness is linked with ideas of completeness, order,

[1] I am convinced by Mary Douglas, *Purity and Danger* (1966), Chapter 3, with one or two very minor modifications.

integrity. To observe the food laws was to express belief in a holy God in a way which, once we understand it, makes sense. The essential step is to go back behind our descriptive zoology to the normative, theological zoologies which came before it. But for centuries this has not been understood.

The Jewish food law is, then, a good example of an ascetical practice which once made sense but later became fossilized and lost its meaning. So it became an easy target for ridicule. If we are to consider Christian asceticism and the charges made against it we must similarly consider the cultural context, the total form of life, within which ascetical practices originally had their proper *rationale*. We said that strong feelings about ascetical practices have often been compounded by ignorance: in considering them we must learn from the anthropologists. For example, in Christian history there has been a very widespread prohibition of nakedness. There are abundant examples of people feeling it right to cover or hide nakedness even when taking a bath, performing copulation, or giving birth to a child. The modern person instantly and perhaps too hastily reacts to this prohibition with ridicule and abhorrence. It would be better first to try to understand it, as a good anthropologist would.

We must also consider the fact that in Jewish and Christian history there has been a very long tradition of criticism of ascetical and cultic practices. The old food laws, and many other rituals which once made sense, became out of date. If there is any justification for *continuing* to observe them in later and different times it cannot be the *same* justification. Observance becomes a way of expressing the continuity of a community. Religious reformers may then attack these old practices because they sense that a new social situation calls for a new kind of religious ordering of experience.

A good example is a parable told by Jesus in Chapter 14 of St. Luke, where people make excuses for declining an invitation to a feast. One must examine his new field, another must try his new oxen, and a third had just married. The point of all this is that in terms of Old Testament ideas of holiness these were all *valid* excuses. Holiness was completeness, totality, perfection. A project left uncompleted was unclean. There was no more sacred obligation than military service, but a man who was in the middle of a project like building a house or marrying was *exempted* even from military service. So the parable says that the eschatological situation which Jesus preached was of such compelling urgency that it overrode the previous religious organization of life and annihilated its authority. Elisha was given time to round things off—to finish with his oxen and take leave of his parents—because the call of Elisha took place *within* the existing religious organization of life. But the disciples of Jesus must drop their projects and abandon everything: the uncleanness incurred does not matter any longer, because Jesus' call dispenses from all previous sacral obligations.

An ascetical system is a religious organization of life: Jesus' call to his disciples supplies a precedent for the annihilation of an entire ascetical system: but also, of course, the basis for the creation of a new one.

An important point of exegesis follows from this consideration. Definitions of asceticism very often make use of such terms as "restraint", "self-discipline" and "renunciation". In Volume One of the *Catholic Dictionary of Theology* (1962), entertainingly subtitled "Abandonment to Casuistry", we find the definition "the practice of self-discipline for the restraint of the passions and advancement in virtue to prepare for union with God by love". The author subordinates asceticism to charity, for he says that "the final purpose of asceticism is the purity of the ordered love of charity", but nevertheless his definition could be misleading. I do not think renunciation ought to be in the foreground in a definition of asceticism. To give an example, virginity is valued in many religions. I do not think that the virgin says: "Sex is good, but God is better still; so I will do without sex in order to think about God all the time." *A fortiori* the virgin does not argue: "Sexual experience is morally or religiously bad, and to be shunned." The point is rather that in many cultures virginity symbolizes a condition of primal innocence, integrity and holiness. A virgin is holy not so much because of any particular horror of sex, as rather for the very same reason that a first-born male lamb, or a heifer, or a new house, or a new cart, might be thought holy, or at least fit for association with the holy. Thus a description of the religious meaning of virginity need not lay emphasis on renunciation or on any pathological fear or moral rejection of sexuality. Reverence for virginity should be related to ways of thinking about the holy in a certain universe of experience. It is certainly mistaken to argue that a high religious valuation of virginity is either necessarily, or always in practice, connected with moral condemnation or emotional abhorrence of sexual experience as such.

Thus Jesus' call to his disciples need not necessarily develop into an ascetical system in which the notion of renunciation is foremost. The disciples are rather exchanging one religious ordering of experience for another. They are leaving behind a world in which it would be somehow defiling to leave the dead unburied, the field half-ploughed, and the fishing-nets half-repaired; and they are entering a world in which God's presence and reality are experienced in a new way. The main emphasis falls not upon what is left behind but upon what is new, the all-overriding claim of God.

So if we are to evaluate Christian asceticism we must ask in the first place about its theological justification. A Christian ascetical form of life is supposed to be determined by, and to express a picture of, the nature of God and his relation to the world and to men. We may ask if it does this successfully, and in a way that *works* for the people who are engaged in it. Then we can ask if there are serious moral objections to it. If there are serious moral objections to a form of life which is thoroughly congruent with Christianity, then a serious moral objection to Christianity itself has become apparent. This is a more profitable way of approaching the subject than the way of crude speculation about the psychology of ascetics which is so popular nowadays.

A word must be said, however, about psychological considerations, particularly those put forward more or less under the aegis of Freud. In his writings, Freud's psychological determinism leads to an almost hydraulic view of the self. There is in every man a bundle of instinctual drives each of which continually seeks and must find some kind of outlet. A drive can quite easily redirect itself: if denied its natural outlet it can find symbolic gratification, or an outlet in fantasy, dreaming or neurosis. But there remains a persisting tendency in Freud to speak in terms of a number of psychic energies at constant pressure.

Freud himself was of course pessimistic: reality is such that all our wishes cannot be gratified, so that we must each learn to endure some measure of instinctual renunciation and the consequent psychic frustration. Thus Freud's name may be invoked in defence of the necessity for everyone of undergoing some kind of ascetical discipline in the battle of life.

More commonly, however, post- or neo-Freudian popular thinking fastens on his early teaching that the neuroses are the result of sexual frustration. Parental or religious prohibitions, internalized in the form of "conscience", become inhibitions associated with intense anxiety and so give rise to neurosis This vulgarization of Freud leads to a strong anti-ascetical climate of opinion. If by asceticism is meant a deliberate attempt to deny any outlet to some or all instinctual drives, and by starving them to weaken them in the hope perhaps of extirpating them altogether—if this is what asceticism means, then popular neo-Freudianism says that it attempts the impossible and the only outcome will be a poisoned and embittered personality.

There is every reason to be sceptical about this popular opinion. It is far from the teaching of Freud himself: it is closer to Rousseau and to the early Romantics. Now savages may be noble, but they are not so in the way Rousseau thought; and Freud himself cared for civilization, and was in no way tempted by sentimental barbarism. I have already suggested that the Freudian or pseudo-Freudian understanding of asceticism is unfruitful and shown to be misleading by modern anthropology. And finally there are nowadays real doubts about the hydraulic model of the self. For example, modern experimental psychology is sceptical about the idea that the varieties of sexual behaviour can be explained by a constant pressure of libidinal energy in each individual, seeking various outlets. Modern studies suggest rather that they are socially learned. The word "instinct" and its cognates are everywhere in retreat nowadays even in the study of animal behaviour: still more in the study of human behaviour.

Such are my reasons for attending primarily to the purported *theological* justifications of Christian asceticism. If Christian asceticism, or some features of it, make rational sense in terms of a certain social world, then psychological arguments are of secondary interest. If by doing this and that I can attain to the vision of God I can contentedly leave psychological speculations to those who are inquisitive about such things.

Now the variety of Christian forms of life has been very great, but our task is made easier by the fact that through most of Christian history, and over most of the Christian world, there has existed something called technically the religious life. So we shall concentrate upon it. To evaluate Christian asceticism adequately we should need to consider *as a whole*, and in context, such documents as the *Rule of St. Benedict*, and many others. That would be a considerable task. More modestly, we shall abstract some of the most widespread common features of Christian asceticism. Though they are best exemplified in the religious life, they have relevance for all Christian life, for in most periods the religious Orders have been the pace-setters. Monks fasted zealously, but the laity too were obliged to fast, though less rigorously. Religious had to obey their superiors, but the laity too in a lesser way were subject to the spiritual jurisdiction of their pastors. Modes of prayer pioneered by the religious eventually were purveyed in a simpler form to the laity. In a small way the layman at the plough or the bench was expected to emulate the monk in his cell. Most Christian ascetical practices are best exemplified among the religious, but were at least known to the laity. Among them are:

1. *Renunciation of property*
Hans von Campenhausen conveniently summarizes the early

Christian teaching,[1] which has remained a constant feature of the Christian life ever since. It is roughly expressed in the classical arrangement whereby the religious lived in poverty, the secular clergy lived in modest circumstances, and the laity were exhorted to give alms generously according to their means. Jesus reportedly vehemently emphasized the moral danger of riches, but refrained from expressly condemning private property as such. But it is clear that a man who answers Jesus' call will not be particularly interested either in accumulating or in holding on to private wealth. He has more interesting things to think about.

Various moral criticisms are made, from different points of view. The renunciation of private property ought not to be commended merely as such. The religious may and usually do own property collectively, and so enjoy considerable security and comfort while at the same time congratulating themselves on their individual poverty. This point has been appreciated in the Christian tradition. In early Franciscan history there was a fierce controversy between the "spirituals" who wished to maintain Francis' own ideals and the "conventuals" who considered the ownership of houses for novice-training and the like inescapable; and most great religious orders have had a history of internal reformation. In Russia in 1503 St. Nilus of Sora opened a similar and fascinating controversy on the ownership of land—and serfs—by monasteries.[2]

A popular objection to the strict renunciation advocated by Nilus and Francis—and also to much Christian almsgiving—is that in a capitalist society the right way to alleviate poverty is to accumulate capital and invest it in order to create more employment and more wealth. Long ago, in a foolish and famous book,[3] Bernard de Mandeville made the point in conscious opposition to the Christian attitude to wealth. He claimed that Christian detachment from riches, if made

[1] "Early Christian Asceticism" in *Tradition and Life in the Church* (1968), E. T. of *Tradition und Leben* (1960).
[2] Good brief account in Timothy Ware, *The Orthodox Church* (1963), pp. 114–118.
[3] *The Fable of the Bees* (the poem published 1705; the book 1714, 1725).

universal, would reduce us to savagery: society depends upon the efforts of the acquisitive entrepreneurs and financiers whom Christian ethics has taught us to despise.

Leslie Stephen[1] thinks this part of Mandeville's argument has real force, but it is clear that he failed to consider that there are alternatives to the Victorian form of capitalism. From the premisses that large accumulations of private wealth are morally dangerous, and that society nevertheless needs to accumulate capital wealth for investment, the conclusion follows that capital should be accumulated by the state or by companies rather than by individuals. A company which is owned by its own workers, for example, might be able to finance its own economic development without there needing to be a class of persons who own substantial private capital and do nothing for a living except lend it out at interest. Alternatively the state can raise capital by taxation. It is not true that a powerful capitalist class is necessary to the social good.

There are certainly moral objections to the practice of Christians in the matter of wealth and poverty, but not I think to the theory. The traditional teaching is much the same as in several other religions, and is entirely capable of reformulation in changed economic circumstances.

2. *Temperance in food and drink*

Fasting has played a large part in Christian asceticism, and the motives for it have not always been particularly edifying. It is not so easy as it might seem to determine Jesus' own attitude, because the Gospel picture of him as constantly feasting, and as being called a "gluttonous man and a wine-bibber" is influenced by the theological motive of showing him as the Messiah. Still, the very fact that the messianic age was foreseen as an age of plenty and of feasting implies that early Christianity did not attach particular importance to fasting. Paul barely mentions the subject, and early Christianity was indifferent or hostile to the old regulations about unclean food, washing before eating, eating only with fellow-believers

---

[1] *English Thought in the Eighteenth Century* (1876), ix, 39.

and the like. Jesus no doubt accepted fasting as a fact, but attached no special importance to it. Von Campenhausen, in the essay cited above, concludes that the early Christian attitude to fasting was not ascetic, and that it was ready on occasion to censure extreme ascetic ideas on the subject.

In later Christian asceticism, however, one finds a much more favourable attitude to fasting. Food and drink, and especially meat and wine, were thought to inflame the passions, and (worst of all) to be aphrodisiac. Because chocolate was thought to be aphrodisiac the Pope once forbade Jesuits to consume it. A man weakened by fasting is more suggestible, and more likely to experience visions and hallucinations. Through fasting, men believed that they would gain mastery over their passions and a greater receptivity to God's influence.

Through much of the Christian tradition one can perceive the influence of the belief that reason should at all times be on her throne and in control of the passions. Any form of emotional release was suspect. Augustine had serious doubts about music: it was only permissible to sing psalms in Church so long as thinking the words took precedence over enjoying the music.[1] He disciplined himself "to take food as medicine" and eat only just enough. Fourteen centuries later Hurrell Froude at Oxford confided to his journal that he had sinned grievously by looking greedily at a roast goose on the High Table.[2]

This absurd scrupulosity has done a great deal of harm and the practice of fasting is now in some disrepute. The Church has lately greatly relaxed its old discipline. There is obvious sense in a reasonable temperance in matters of food and drink, and in protest against the monumental gluttony of Trimalchio's banquet.[3] But there is no good reason, in terms of Christian theology, for supposing that the sight of a voluntarily hungry man is pleasanter to God than the sight of a man adequately fed. Belief in the value of fasting, as in the case of many other ascetical practices, was supported by a doctrine about reason

[1] *Confessions*, X, 33.
[2] *Remains*, Volume 1 (1838).
[3] Described in the *Satyricon* of Petronius.

and the passions to which Plato had lent his authority. But the doctrine was fallacious. Plato imagined a thirsty man presented with a cup of water, and suggested that passion says "Drink", whereas reason says "Wait: it may be poisoned."[1] But the real conflict here is between a desire to quench one's thirst and a desire not to be poisoned. Plato's doctrine suggested that a rational ethic will always be an ethic of deferred or postponed enjoyments, and that there is something irrational about any spontaneously enjoyed pleasure. Incorporated into Christian asceticism, it produced an odiously calculating temperament, incapable of immediate feeling and enjoyment. And as Plato's supposed conflict between the passions and reason is really a conflict between two passions, so, when adopted into Christian asceticism, it represented as a victory of reason what was too often really a victory of self-disgust over natural affection.

3. *Submission of the will to the direction of ecclesiastical superiors*

The discipline of obedience required in most Western forms of the religious life might be thought at first glance one of its most obviously objectionable features. In fact it needs handling with care. Its purpose was clearly disciplinary: the Benedictine Abbot, for example, was elected by a free vote of the fully-professed monks. They *gave* him his authority over them: he was not like a Tibetan Lama. It might be thought that if they could elect their abbot, the monks might for once simply fail to elect him, and conduct all their subsequent business democratically. But anyone familiar with the religious life knows that many of those who pray a great deal become very obstinate and intransigent personalities. The emphasis on the Superior's authority may be seen as a checking device. Students of Church history are aware that monks have not been exactly timorous, broken men: without the rule of their superiors they would doubtless have been still more quarrelsome and determined. Benedict's Rule created a singularly enduring society: there is undoubtedly a great deal of practical shrewdness in it. But that shrewdness is in turn itself morally questionable: it might be that by taking away from a man the

[1] *Republic*, IV, 434D–441C.

habit of making his own decisions you can institutionalize him very effectively. He will not leave the society because he has become unfitted for life outside it. The mere endurance of a religious society does not prove that all the devices which have made it durable are *morally* admirable. So you could look at the phenomena from a hostile point of view, like this: people thought the religious life, in societies, a good thing. But it makes men quarrelsome and obstinate. So the government of the societies was made highly authoritarian, and they were turned in on themselves to exclude any contaminating contact with the outside world. This ensured the survival of the societies: but perhaps the initial assumption that the societies were a good thing was mistaken?

The traditional monarchical pattern of government in Christian institutions at all levels has been under fire at least since the time when Luther broke with the Pope. The continuance of these monarchical patterns, after monarchical rule has largely disappeared from secular institutions, is a chronic scandal. It was associated with belief in the monarchy of God, the unity of truth, and the belief that the Church was the sole trustee and sole authoritative interpreter of a body of revealed truths. But leaving aside cultural considerations, there was always a theological objection. The extrinsic rule of a spiritual superior over a man's conscience is not and never was a good analogy for the soul's relation to God. For God does not tell me what to do in the way that another man may do. He leaves me to make up my own mind: he gives me guidance perhaps, but, even then, it is I who choose to regard it as such. The way the Pope, in a notorious recent encyclical, directed the consciences of the married Catholic laity is in no way like the way in which God guides the Christian man in making moral decisions. The total submission of the will to ecclesiastical superiors is in the last resort a *theologically* objectionable notion, because it implies an extrinsic picture of God as a wise and benevolent *despot*. And God is not like a despot because he does not issue and enforce legislation like an earthly despot: only a primitive and superstitious theology can suppose that he does.

41

4. *Sexual asceticism*

The Christian tradition of sexual asceticism also needs to be discussed with care, and the subject is of immense complexity. I have already suggested that a reverence for virginity is by no means necessarily or always associated with abhorrence of sexuality. If we look at the social context in which virginity is reverenced we may well find that it is believed holy, or fit for association with the holy, for the same reason that the first sheaf harvested, or a newly-finished building, are apt for dedication to God. There is something special about a ship's maiden voyage or the discovery of virgin territory which makes special ceremonies seem appropriate. Many feel that old landscapes and even old townscapes should be left unspoiled and not "raped" by bulldozers. Thus reverence for virginity may represent simply the application to the sexual realm of a general notion of the holy and its expression in social structures.

But a critic can still say with justice that a special esteem for virginity, like a special reverence for virgin forest, belongs better with pre-Christian than with Christian theology. So far as we can tell from the Gospels, Jesus was not particularly interested in sexual asceticism, and the general point still holds that his eschatological message annihilates the previous highly-elaborated religious organization of life. In the Levitical organization of life, in which holiness was linked with integrity and clear boundaries, any discharge from the body incurred ceremonial uncleanness. Even menstruation was surrounded by elaborate rituals. It is not the purpose of these rituals to inculcate a horror of sex, but, as I have insisted, to express in social life a vision of the holy. Nevertheless, it is also clear that early Christianity, in breaking with the old ideas of cleanness and uncleanness, was committed in the long run to a very different way of working out its theology in social life. The case against much Christian sexual asceticism is that it fell back into earlier patterns which were out of keeping with Christian theology. In connexion with the Lenten fast, Eastern Christian asceticism could devise food laws as elaborate as the Jewish, in spite of the fact that the Lord had declared all foods clean. And, correspondingly, Western Christians still sing with enthusiasm the old monastic compline *Te lucis ante terminum* in which they pray to be delivered from nocturnal "pollution". The belief that the emission of semen creates a condition of impurity is part of the Levitical code,[1] but its presence in a Christian context is incongruous. When in the rule of St. Benedict we read how carefully the brethren were to be secluded from any casual contact with outsiders, and from any contact at all with excommunicates,[2] we feel that this is incongruous in followers of Jesus, who on the early Christians' testimony positively sought and relished the company of such persons. And similarly, leaving aside emotional and psychological considerations, much Christian sexual asceticism leaves one with the same feeling of incongruity.

Why in a Christian milieu has it been so firmly believed that Jesus was virginally conceived, that Mary remained virgin even after parturition, that Mary remained virgin for life, that John the Baptist and Jesus were unmarried, that all or most of the early disciples and apostles were unmarried or abandoned their wives, that celibacy is of the essence of the religious life, that either the higher clergy or all clergy ought to be celibates, and so on? The grounds adducible in support of these beliefs scarcely justify the tenacity with which they have been held. One of the unanswered questions of history is what Gregory of Nyssa's wife thought of his treatise *On Virginity*, in which the saint asserts that earthly marriage is quite incompatible with spiritual advancement, that virginity is the foundation of all virtues, that a virgin soul resembles God, and then eloquently laments his own marriage.

There have been many attempts to explain how this happened. The favourite suggestion is that in the earliest period celibacy was related to the expectation that the Kingdom of God was imminent. Celibacy was thus part of an interim-ethic dominated by eschatology. Later the eschatological perspective was lost, but celibacy persisted because in the Hellenistic world it was thought meritorious in itself. I have doubts about this explanation. Jeremiah's celibacy was

[1] Leviticus 15:16.
[2] Rules 26 and 66.

determined by his belief that God's judgement would be coming soon and would be very unpleasant. Wives and children will "die of dreadful diseases".[1] But later Jews and Christians took a more cheerful view of the Kingdom of God. Why in any case should the nearness of the kingdom of God be thought a good reason for inactivity? When war is declared many men want to beget a child before they are killed: I am not convinced that it is right that, in the interim period between the declaration that the End is nigh and the coming of the End, everything must grind to a halt and everyone must wait with bated breath. Many people who learn that they have an incurable illness decide to pack the time they have left with as much moral action and enjoyment of life as they can. Is that not just as reasonable? Why should the nearness and inevitability of the Parousia be a reason for inaction rather than for action?

The answer, I suppose, is that it was indeed a reason for action, but action of one kind only. Preaching the Kingdom not merely took precedence over all else, but replaced all else. St. Paul puts the matter with great simplicity: "the unmarried man is anxious about the affairs of the Lord, how to please the Lord; but the married man is anxious about worldly affairs, how to please his wife, and his interests are divided."[2]

There are great difficulties of exegesis here (which is a learned way of saying that St. Paul contradicts himself) and C. K. Barrett notices some of them in his *Commentary*.[3] Why should God (or, I would add, his spouse) be a source of anxiety to the Christian, who, the Apostle has just said, is supposed to be free from anxiety (*amerimnous*)? Why does Paul imply that unmarried women are specially "holy in body" (v. 34), when elsewhere he says that all Christian bodies are holy? Yet though he sees these difficulties, and although he is conspicuously a Protestant exegete, Barrett can still conclude that "the prime misfortune of the married man . . . is that his mind is divided." But why? The presumption appears to be that the acts by which one pleases God are a quite separate

[1] Jeremiah 16: 2–4 (RSV).
[2] 1 Corinthians 7: 32–34 (RSV).
[3] 1968, pp. 178–180.

44

class of acts from moral duties such as the acts whereby one pleases a spouse. This presumption was regarded by Socrates and Kant, and many Biblical writers, as the very essence of superstition. A spouse is at least a neighbour, and Christianity has always said that its moral ideal is the expression of love for the neighbour and for God in a single, identical, undivided act. If in the belief that they are rivals I turn away from my neighbour to God, I turn away from Christianity.

Nevertheless, St. Paul's error here became bound up in Christian asceticism with the ladder-mysticism of contemporary Hellenism. To the scale of being there corresponds a scale of loving, Augustine's *ordo amoris*. On the lower rungs the soul loves God through creatures, but on the highest rungs the soul loves God for himself alone. The intensity with which a thing should be loved must correspond with its dignity in the scale of being. This detestable doctrine, with which Christian mysticism has almost always been entangled, projects upon the universe the same spirit as that which leads snobs to esteem dukes higher than dustmen. Its ideal is Gregory of Nyssa's: the soul becomes a solitary, uncontaminated virgin, contemplating a God who is the same.

5. *Vigilance*

Much of what I would wish to say about this feature of Christian asceticism has been said already in other contexts, but I will not leave it without some comment. Religious writing with a strong eschatological flavour very often emphasizes the virtues of sobriety and vigilance. The believer must keep his wits about him so that he does not mistake or fail to notice the significant event when it occurs.

In Christian asceticism this theme is joined with another: the persistence of sinful desires in the believer. The Christian is surrounded by demons who are attempting to lure him into committing some sin. Naturally the lure is speciously attractive. Thus everything beautiful or desirable may be seen as a potential occasion of sin, and to be shunned. Temptation comes not only through the five senses, but still more insidiously, through thoughts. Thus no object that is presented to sense or comes to

45

mind can be enjoyed or contemplated as it is, until it has under-gone an anxious scrutiny to see whether there is not some lurk-ing wickedness in it. So what was at first a vigilant looking for the Lord's coming developed into an habitual and rigorous self-examination and even a morbid introspectiveness.

Various elements contributed to this tradition: the constant recitation of the 119th Psalm, the influence of Book X of Augustine's *Confessions*, the representation of the spiritual life as a constant struggle against demons, the Church's developing penitential discipline, and others. Its psychological influence has outlasted its overt acknowledgement; and has been, among the laity, quite as strong in Protestantism as in Catholicism.

Its strengths ought not to go unnoticed. It realized in many of the key men in European history an intense self-awareness and a creative capacity for spiritual struggle. This is strikingly true of such men as Paul, Augustine, Luther, Pascal, Kierke-gaard, and Newman. Such men were intensely self-conscious and *dramatic* characters, for whom the sinful soul's relation to God mattered above all else: they were men capable of gripping autobiographical writing.

But the cost in mental anguish was very great, and the *anxiety* of such men is in many ways incongruent with Christian faith. The tendency to fall back into morbid scrupulosity has been very strong in the history of Christian thought, and very hard to banish.

And now a final observation. If there has been a morbid and intropunitive strain in Christian asceticism, whence did it come? Perhaps from a misreading of the Gospels. For the Gos-pels say that Jesus predicted his own Passion and death at Jerusalem, and they also say that he voluntarily chose to go there. The inference is hard to avoid: Jesus must have volun-tarily and knowingly chosen and sought the way of suffering and death. A true disciple should do the same.

This was a misunderstanding: the Gospels see Jesus with the benefit of hindsight, and they ascribe to the earthly Jesus divine powers such as foreknowledge, proper to the Christ worshipped by the Early Church. Imitating Jesus need not imply seeking pain: the message is rather that if life's sorrows are met Christianly they may *in retrospect* be seen as having had valuable effects. And the Early Church did in fact discourage the voluntary courting of martyrdom. Since the Gospels seem to say that Jesus did court martyrdom, and that one ought to imitate him by taking up a cross like his, the Early Church must (if it was to resist the inference) have grasped something of the nature of a Gospel. It must have realized that a Gospel is written with hindsight, and that it is only *in retrospect* that suffering can (sometimes) be seen as redemptive and accepted as such. It should not be actively sought.

But where this point was *not* grasped it could seem that the most whole-hearted follower of Jesus ought to imitate him by seeking pain. Many saints did. Nevertheless, common sense, like cheerfulness, keeps breaking in. In his autobiography *The Life of the Servant*, Henry Suso, a pupil of Eckhart, describes how for sixteen years he tormented himself with a hair shirt, manacles, and various other instruments of self-torture. Finally, "one Whitsunday a host of angels appeared to him in a vision, and announced that God did not wish him to continue. Then he desisted, and threw everything into the river."[1]

We began with two possibilities: either traditional patterns of Christian asceticism are congruous with Christian theism, or they are not. If they are, then moral objections to them are moral objections to Christian theism itself. However, I have argued that much in the traditional ascetical disciplines is morally objectionable at just the points where it is not true to Christian theism. Too much in it was a lapse from Christian theism back to earlier patterns of religious thought.

[1] Trans. J. M. Clark (1952), p. 47.

3

HAS CHRISTIANITY REINFORCED
THE SUBJECTION OF WOMEN?

A MORAL criticism of Christianity which has not yet received sufficient attention is that it has always taught male primacy, and so has contributed to and reinforced the age-long subjection of women.[1] Ever since the French Revolution women have compared their lot with that of other oppressed groups, such as negroes,[2] or the working class; and it has seemed to them that in their case also religion has been used as an opiate, a device for deflecting their attention from their grievances, and teaching them resignation to their allotted destiny. Men make Gods, and women worship them: and among the gods the male is naturally supreme, and even solitary in his supremacy. The archetypal believer is pictured as a docile and obedient woman,

[1] The following are some of the principal relevant works: Mary Wollstonecraft, *A Vindication of the Rights of Women* (1790) and John Stuart Mill, *The Subjection of Women* (1869), printed together in Everyman's Library 825 (latest printing 1965); introduction to American history, with documents, in W. L. O'Neill, *The Woman Movement* (1969); British history, in Ray Strachey, *The Cause* (1929). See also Ethel Mannin, *Women and the Revolution* (1938); Simone de Beauvoir, *Le Deuxiéme Sex* (1949)—the paperback ET of the first part of this is entitled *A History of Sex* (i.e. Women), (New English Library, 1968); Betty Friedan, *The Feminine Mystique* (1963), often reprinted by Penguin books; and the most bloodcurdling diatribe of all, Valerie Solanas, *The SCUM Manifesto* (New York 1968). There is at present a minor explosion of books, for example S. F. Epstein, *Woman's Place* (1970); Eva Figes, *Patriarchal Attitudes* (1970); Germaine Greer, *The Female Eunuch* (1970). Classical sources include the Bible; Aristotle, *On the Generation of Animals* (Volume V of the Smith-Ross edition, 1912); Augustine, *The City of God*, Books XII–XIV; St. Thomas Aquinas, *Summa Theologiae*. Theologians, in D. S. Bailey, *The Man-Woman Relation in Christian Thought* (1959); E. Troeltsch, *The Social Teaching of the Christian Churches* (ET 1931). Many of these books are cited hereafter by the author's name and a page-number.

[2] Consider, for example, that a London secretary is called a Girl-Friday, a neat example of "sexual racism"; and that, in American universities, Departments of Women's Studies arrived just after Departments of Black Studies.

48

the symbol of the Church. In such a context a feminist revolt is a revolt against religion.

Feminism was born of the Enlightenment, of the same sort of forces which produced the moral philosophy of Kant. The French Revolution created a climate in which it could gain a hearing. Soon after the National Assembly had published its Declaration of the Rights of Man, Olympe de Gouges proposed a *Declaration of the Rights of Women*.[1] If the Revolution could free negro slaves and confer citizenship upon Jews, why should women be excluded? But they *were* excluded, and the lot of women was made worse by the *Code Napoléon*. The Emperor, like those other distinguished military men, Stalin and Hitler, saw women as patriotic producers of cannon-fodder.

In England, Mary Wollstonecraft was writing while her husband William Godwin was completing his great *Enquiry Concerning Political Justice* (1793). Godwin saw marriage as a property relation, a kind of slavery. Only with its abolition could women recover their moral dignity. Mary Wollstonecraft is willing to describe marriage in the phrase, "legalized prostitution". The official morality ensures that the only moral difference between a good woman and a bad is that a good woman does not cheapen herself, but regards herself as an expensive commodity to be attractively packaged and cunningly sold for a high price, whereas a bad woman prices herself too low. A woman's virtue is her skill in playing the market. The observation still seemed startling when the Communist Manifesto appeared fifty years later,[2] and it seemed startling even when Bernard Shaw made hostile remarks about the London marriage market over a century later.[3] Yet the justice of it should be apparent to anyone who reads Samuel Richardson's *Pamela* (1740), a truly shocking novel in that the author is seemingly all unconscious of the morality of the tale he tells.

[1] Published in 1789.

[2] The classic treatment of the subject is Engels' *The Origin of the Family, Private Property and the State*. See also Karl Marx, *Economic and Philosophic Manuscripts of 1844*, ed. D. J. Struick (1964), p. 134.

[3] E.g. "Capitalism acts on women as a continual bribe to enter into sex relations for money, whether in or out of marriage", from *The Intelligent Woman's Guide to Socialism*; and the play, *Mrs Warren's Profession*.

Anarchism helped Mary Wollstonecraft see her way more clearly. Mill remarks that: "By the old laws of England, the husband was called the *lord* of the wife; he was literally regarded as her sovereign, inasmuch that the murder of a man by his wife was called treason (*petty* as distinguished from *high* treason), and was more cruelly avenged than was usually the case with high treason, for the penalty was burning to death."[1] Anarchism, rebelling against the great monarchy of kings, was bound to extend its principles to the little monarchy of husbands and fathers.

But the strongest, most unanswerable part of Mary Wollstonecraft's case was her appeal to the unity of virtue. Men were none too clear whether women were human, moral beings, or creatures intermediate between men and faithful domestic animals. In practice it seemed the latter: the virtues recommended to women were "gentleness, docility, and a spaniel-like affection"; "she was created to be the toy of man, his rattle, and it must jingle in his ears whenever, dismissing reason, he chooses to be amused."[2] But many men oscillate between contempt for women and adoration of them: women were also called angels (a metaphor common at least up to the time of Coventry Patmore) and angels are not supposed to be less rational than men. Their religion teaches men that women are capable of salvation, and of virtue. But if women are moral beings, subject to the same eternal standard of virtue, how can there be virtues specific to one sex or the other? Mary Wollstonecraft recognizes that there may be distinction of sex-roles: "Women, I allow, may have different duties to fulfil; but they are *human* duties, and the principles that should regulate the discharge of them, I sturdily maintain, must be the same."[3] She will even allow that men may *exceed* women in virtue: but it does not follow from this that they should pursue *different* virtues. And she also points out that from the historical fact (if it be a fact) that women *have* always been subject it does not follow that they *ought* always to remain so.

[1] Mill, 246.
[2] Wollstonecraft, 38.
[3] Wollstonecraft, 57.

In what follows I shall concede all this: that is, I allow that women are moral beings as men are, and that they ought to enjoy the same moral liberty and moral respect as men. And it is a fact that in Christianity the common teaching has been that "sex is not in the soul",[1] and that women may be admitted to the sacraments and to public worship on the same terms as men. Certainly this has been part of Christian teaching: the question is whether or not Christianity has added such qualifications as in effect to subvert its basic teaching, and so connived at and reinforced the degradation of women.

It should of course be clear that we are not here concerned with whether Christianity is or is not hostile to human sexuality. Nor am I discussing the theology of marriage. These are different questions. We are rather asking how far, and for what reasons, Christianity has joined Moses, Aristotle and Freud in being androcentric—treating the male as the normal and standard human being and the female as eccentric, deviant or defective; and arguing that the female exists only to serve the male, and should live under his rule.

Here are four topics discussed by feminists which illustrate the question. *First*, does the Bible itself teach the supremacy of the male? Many early feminists thought that God must surely be egalitarian. Sarah Grimké, an American feminist, endeavoured to defend herself against a bevy of Congregationalist ministers in her *Letters on the Equality of the Sexes* (1838). She believed that the Bible does teach the moral equality of the sexes, and that it is morally wrong to put a woman down by telling her that there are certain virtues, such as modesty and delicacy, to be cultivated by her sex only.[2] Ten years later the Seneca Falls Convention of 1848 first charged the Church with being a stronghold of androcentrism: "He [i.e. man] allows her in Church, as well as in State, but a subordinate position, claiming Apostolic authority for her exclusion from the ministry." But for this not the Scriptures themselves, but "a perverted application of the Scriptures" was blamed.[3]

[1] *Summa Theologiae*, III, Supp. 39, art. 1.
[2] Quoted in O'Neill, 103ff.
[3] O'Neill, 109–11.

Throughout Jewish and Christian history theologians and their critics have alike attended to the second, more primitive creation story which describes Eve being made from Adam's rib, rather than to the first, which describes God as making the two sexes together. Since the primacy and supremacy of the male was taken for granted in ancient culture, the theologians[1] felt it hardly needed any more justification than a brief reference to this story. It has only in recent times been customary to hold that the image of God resides equally in either sex, or resides in the community of both sexes together. The common assumption, at least in the West, has been that the male is made in the image of God, and the female participates in the image of God via the male.[2] Vigorous male supremacists like John Milton are quite clear that there is an analogy; as God to the male, so the male to the female:

> Hee for God only, Shee for God in him . . . [3]

And still more brazenly, Milton's Eve is made to say to Adam:

> My author and disposer, what thou bidst
> Unargued I obey; so God ordains,
> God is thy law, thou mine: to know no more
> Is woman's happiest knowledge and her praise.[4]

Milton makes Adam protest about this arrangement.[5] For Adam tells Raphael that though she is not so clever as he is, whenever he *does* have an argument with Eve, she always seems to be in the right. Raphael rebukes Adam firmly, and tells him that male supremacy is God's law. To this Adam replies, in effect, "It's all right for you—what do you know about it?"— and Raphael has the grace to blush.[6]

What the feminists think of Milton it would be unkind to that

[1] For the status of women in early Christianity see Bailey, 61–69. The classic definition of the female as an "impotent male" in Aristotle, 728a; and in Aquinas, *ST* I, 92, art. 1.

[2] But see Gregory of Nyssa, *On the Making of Man*, XVI. The image of God is imprinted prior to the differentiation of the two sexes: there is a trace of the idea of an original androgyne in Greek theology.

[3] *Paradise Lost*, IV, 299.

[4] *ibid.*, 635–8.

[5] See Adam's remarks to God *before* Eve's creation in VIII, 380–92.

[6] *ibid.*, VIII, 540–620. See William Empson, *Milton's God* (1965 edn.), pp. 104f.

great man's memory to recount;[1] but it is clear that by the later nineteenth century women conceded that the Bible *does* teach male supremacy. Mary Wollstonecraft had simply said that the story of Adam's rib is a fable.[2] Elizabeth Cady Stanton even published a *Woman's Bible*, suitably amended, on the ground that since Higher Criticism had shown that human frailty has influenced the writing of Scripture it is right to expurgate Holy Writ of its grosser immoralities, the doctrine of male supremacy being the chief. Modern feminists take it for granted that "God is a male chauvinist" to quote the title of a leaflet,[3] and that St. Paul was, if not a misogynist, certainly a male supremacist. Simone de Beauvoir epitomizes the common verdict[4] in saying that "Christian ideology has contributed no little to the oppression of women". It was not at first misogynous: "there is in the Gospel a breath of charity that extends to women as to lepers." Women clung to the new Faith and were honoured when they died for it. But "through St. Paul the Jewish tradition, savagely anti-feminist, was affirmed". Christian theology imposed a threefold subjection on women (and here I am tidying up Mme. de Beauvoir): first, she is subject to man even prior to the Fall in being made from man for man;[5] secondly, because she was most to blame for the Fall, in consequence of it her subjection has been made servile—she really is man's serf;[6] and, finally, the last shackles were fastened upon her by St. Paul's Christological argument for male supremacy.[7] Later, under the influence of patristic asceticism, an open and ugly misogyny appeared. The oppression of women became a positive duty. As the occasion of the first sin, woman began to

[1] "There appears in his books something like a Turkish contempt of females", says Dr. Johnson in his *Life of Milton*.

[2] Wollstonecraft, 30.

[3] *New Statesman*, May 1, 1970.

[4] *History of the Second Sex*, Part 2, cc. 4 and 5.

[5] Gen. 2: 21–23; 1 Cor. 11: 7–9 (but contrast 1 Cor. 7: 2–5, which teaches a reciprocal rule).

[6] Gen. 3:16; see *Summa Theologiae* I, 92, art. 1, reply to Obj. 2, for the two kinds of subjection.

[7] Eph. 5: 22. That there *is* a Christological argument for male supremacy here is disputed by some modern exegetes. See the article by Willy Rordorf, "Marriage in the New Testament and in the Early Church", *Journal of Ecclesiastical History*, XX, no. 2, October 1969, pp. 193ff.

typify all sin: she was temptation incarnate. Most Western theologians since Augustine have held that the way we experience sexual desire and pleasure has been radically tainted by the Fall. Thus the form of our sexual feeling is the empirical evidence of the truth of the doctrine of Original Sin:[1] to repress and restrict women is to enact visibly and symbolically the repression of inordinate sexual feeling within oneself, because it is women who occasion that feeling. Subjugating Eve without, a man conquers the old Adam within. So "the Christian's attitude towards God, the world and his own flesh was reflected in the situation to which he consigned (woman)".[2] To seclude women, and stop them running free, is to keep sex in its place, because women *are* sex. To this day some Anglicans argue that women in the pulpit or in the sanctuary means "sex" (mysterious word) in the sanctuary. And Christianity inherited from Judaism a belief that women are, or are at certain seasons, ceremonially unclean, as is shown by the long tradition of a purification-rite after childbirth.

And I am not digressing here: for if we ask, *why* does the God of the Bible have no consort, *why* is he so relentlessly male, the answer is not easy to discover. There are perhaps traces of an earlier matriarchy in Genesis:[3] there are one or two lines in the Second Isaiah applying female imagery to God,[4] but otherwise patriarchy is unmitigated.[5] Probably the reason is that God began life as a warrior, and warriors must have nothing to do with women, who make a man weak and unclean. I shall suggest a larger reason why God has been described in predominantly masculine imagery later.

A *second* strand in the feminist case is one that has been very little noticed: the curiously intense way in which women ex-

[1] Augustine was led, says Bailey very justly (55), "to a virtual equation of original sin, concupiscence and venereal emotion".
[2] De Beauvoir, 153.
[3] The patriarchs "go in to" their women's tents, and Jacob (Genesis 24:67) appears to take his wife to his mother's tent, a trace of "matrilocal residence".
[4] Isaiah 49:15.
[5] The Hebrew vocabulary shows it: a man "takes" a woman in marriage, and the woman "is for" the man. As in most languages the vocabulary of generation is agricultural: *seed, fertile, barren* (the last two being predicated *only* of women in the Old Testament).

perienced the problem of evil in the nineteenth century. Mary Wollstonecraft asks God if he has created women for no better purpose than to be men's playthings.[1] But the longest English statement is by Florence Nightingale, who recorded her spiritual struggles in a long confessional book *Suggestions for Thought*, written in 1852 and still unpublished. Into it she poured out her thoughts on religion and the woman question, for, as Ray Strachey says, "Her thoughts of God and his justice must be made to square with his treatment of her sex."[2] "Why have women passion, intellect, moral activity", she asks, "and a place in society where none of the three can be exercised?"[3] The nineteenth century was, for men, an age of strenuous moral activity. The old Christianity of resignation had given place to a new Christianity of good works. But women remained stuck in the old faith, sentenced to self-denial, and men, as always, were angry with them if they said they were unhappy. Women had to deny that they had any sexual feeling, they could not exercise their bodies, use their minds, own property, or engage in any public business. They must fritter away their lives in domestic pastimes. And this was God's law, and the Church praised women who submitted to it. The most humane, reasonable and authoritative of all theologians, St. Thomas Aquinas, says that when God made woman to help man he meant, *solely* in the work of generation, because for every other purpose another man would have been a better help.[4]

According to a great Freudian maxim, "anatomy is destiny",[5] and for Freud no woman can overcome the handicap of being a woman. Psychoanalysis seeks to liberate men for action, but to teach women to renounce feminist cravings and to submit to their destiny without bitterness.[6] Every woman's basic neurosis is a futile longing to be a man, and she must overcome it.

And *that* is what women were and are bitter about. It is what

[1] 74f.
[2] Strachey, 26. An extract from Florence Nightingale's book appears in an Appendix.
[3] Strachey, 396.
[4] *Summa Theologiae* I, 92, art. 1.
[5] *Collected Papers* II (1924), p. 274.
[6] *Collected Papers* V (1950), pp. 354ff.

Lucy Stone meant in 1855: "In education, in marriage, in religion, in everything, disappointment is the lot of woman."[1] At about the same time Florence Nightingale actually dreamt of herself as a female John the Baptist,[2] preparing the way for "a female Christ" . . . "who will resume in her own soul the sufferings of her race".[3]

Here is another American, M. Carey Thomas, Principal of Bryn Mawr College, looking back on her early struggles:

> I read the Bible entirely through with passionate eagerness, because I had heard it said that it proved that women were inferior to men. I can remember weeping over the account of Adam and Eve because it seemed to me that the curse pronounced on Eve might imperil girls' going to college; and to this day I can never read many parts of the Pauline epistles without feeling again the sinking of the heart with which I used to hurry over the verses referring to women's keeping silence in the churches . . . I read Milton with rage and indignation. Even as a child I knew him for the woman hater he was . . . I was terror-struck lest I, and every other woman with me, were doomed to live as pathological invalids in a universe merciless to woman as a sex.[4]

A *third* strand in the feminist case against Christianity is of course the exclusion of women from the Ministry. The first religious body to give equal standing to the sexes was the Salvation Army, whose regulations state that "the Army refuses to make any difference between men and women as to rank, authority and duties". The steadfast maintenance of this principle has been a notable factor in the Army's success, and the case is all the more remarkable because it is often said that Protestantism, placing less emphasis on Mary, is more androcentric and suspicious of women than Catholicism.[5]

The first great period of feminism ended about 1919, when the Pope pronounced in favour of votes for women, and the Removal of Sex Disqualification Act was passed in England. These events reminded people that though there had been nineteenth-century

[1] Friedan, 80.
[2] Strachey, 395, title and motto.
[3] Strachey, 414, 416.
[4] O'Neill, 169.
[5] Almost all Protestant churches have now admitted the ordination of women, at least in principle. The Congregationalists were the first.

broad-churchmen like Kingsley who supported feminism, the profession of Orders was still closed to women. The 1920s saw the first serious agitation: C. E. Raven was a well-known advocate. But, though Hensley Henson remarked on the number of bishops at the Lambeth Conference who were feminists,[1] the Church has behaved rather like Henry James' Lord Warburton in holding progressive opinions without thought of applying them to itself. And Henson's own statement conveys just the right nuance of repugnance: "The world wants desperately not female priests and bishops but Christian wives and mothers."[2] One is reminded of Samuel Johnson on women preachers.

Among the Documents of the Second Vatican Council there are a number of sympathetic references to the question of women's rights,[3] including one urging that they should play a greater part in the apostolate. But no woman was a member of that enormous body, though by the end of its deliberations there were present twenty-two "auditrices"—*listeners*. And it has never been explained satisfactorily why a woman can be a capable and respected minister in the Government, but not in the Church. Aquinas struggles unsuccessfully to explain why a woman may be a sovereign, or a prophet, but not a priest.[4] His reply is exceptionally feeble, and certainly suggests that woman's status is lowered by redemption, if indeed she *may* be superior in the order of nature, but *must* be inferior in the order of grace. (Aquinas of course holds that men would have ruled other men in paradise. On his neoplatonist presuppositions a society in which one rules another is more varied and valuable than one in which two are equal.) But, if Aquinas is right, redemption *lowers* the dignity of women, a theologically astounding conclusion.[5]

---

[1] *Retrospect of an Unimportant Life*, II (1943), p. 6. For Anglican feminism in the 1920s, compare the 1662 and 1928 marriage services in the BCP.

[2] See E. M. Lang, *British Women in the Twentieth Century*, (1929), p. 137.

[3] See W. M. Abbott, *Documents of Vatican II* (1965), Index, s.v. "women".

[4] *Summa Theologiae* III, 39, art. 1. Compare Hooker (cited above) *Ecclesiastical Policy*, V, 62, 2. Note his quotation from the *Apostolic Constitutions* about the impious Greeks "which for the service of women goddesses have women priests".

[5] The lamentable Anglican history can be traced through the bibliography to *Women and Holy Orders* (1966), published by the Church Information Office. The aptest summary of it is the *mot* "Praejudicium quaerens intellectum", for which we are indebted to G. W. H. Lampe. See, for example, K. E. Kirk, "The Ordination of Women", in *Beauty and Bands* (1955).

The *fourth* and last strand to be mentioned appears in the revival of feminism in the 1960s. In the 1920s classical feminism declined. Women were by and large achieving the legislative changes they desired.[1] There was a feeling of anticlimax, and there were ideological disputes, as over the question whether legislation should simply be sex-blind or whether there should be special protective legislation to prevent the exploitation of female labour. In general, women felt that it was now up to them to make use of their new freedoms. It was only much later that women, like the blacks, found that legislation was not enough. By the 1960s it became clear that the position of women was actually deteriorating.

For example, the income-gap between American men and women in full-time employment was wider in 1968 than it had been in 1957. The figures, according to *Time* magazine[2] are:

	1957	1968
men	$4713	$7800
women	$3008	$4550

Blacks appear now to be earning more than women. Their average annual income remained from 1957 to 1967 static as a proportion of white income at about 70%.[3] More recently there have been reports that black incomes are rising relatively, as well as absolutely. So that while black Americans are perhaps getting better off, women are certainly getting worse off. What is more, lower black incomes may be explained (though not justified) by saying that most blacks come from poorer homes, and so forth; whereas this cannot be said when comparing men with women. And it is not true that women work only for "pin-money". In the U.S.A., two-thirds of women workers work from necessity, and over one-third of the poorest families have no man.

It is notorious that the number of women in the American House of Representatives, and in European Parliaments, has

[1] But they only won the vote in France after the Second World War.
[2] November 21, 1969, p. 57.
[3] John Vincent, *The Race Race* (1970), p. 35.

tended to decline rather than to increase in recent decades. Both in America and in Britain[1] the proportion of women among University students and staff has declined steadily for generations.[2]

Why has this happened? In a word, the reason why 70% of Russian doctors, but only 7% of American doctors, are women must be cultural. And it is obviously true that many of the most influential minds of the modern period have been strongly anti-feminist. It is sufficient to mention the names of Schopenhauer, Nietzsche, Kierkegaard, Strindberg, Lawrence (the twentieth century's Rousseau), and, above all, Freud. All, except perhaps Lawrence, were also misogynists.[3]

The neo-feminists argue that since the 1920s the influence of biology upon the contemporary picture of human nature—especially, but by no means only, through Freud,—helped society to take its revenge upon the old feminists. They were now ridiculed as *un*feminine, and women were persuaded that biological fulfilment must be their first goal: they must seek sexual emancipation, not social emancipation.[4] The very striking sexual hedonism of modern culture has brought about a kind of "New Victorianism", and a revival of natural-law arguments for the subjection of women. The old *Küche, Kinder, Kirche* ethos was revived in an updated, more hedonistic form, and women

---

[1] Evidence in the Robbins Report. See also Fabian Research Pamphlet 268, *Equality for Women* (1968), for detailed information about the present position of women in the U.K.

[2] The loss to religious thought may be gauged from this table, extracted from the *Cambridge Reporter* for June 17, 1970, reporting "O" and "A" level examination results:

	Number of boys	% passes	Number of girls	% passes
"O level Bible Knowledge	1722	43.3	4586	63.6
"A" level Divinity	107	56.1	493	71.8

In University-level theology the girls are a small minority, but they still do better.

[3] For Freud's misogyny, P. Rieff, *Freud: The Mind of the Moralist* (1960), Chapter V. Freud was hostile to women analysts! There have recently been attempts to right the harmful effects of orthodox psychoanalysis upon women: e.g. K. Horney, *Feminine Psychology* (1967). Freud is a bogey to the neo-feminists, who point to his erroneous views about female orgasm.

[4] Andrew Sinclair, *The Better Half* (1965).

were trapped in the home again, but this time with machines instead of servants for company. Through advertising and the mass media the popular image of woman was changed back again into the brainless, fluffy plaything, the nymphet. Garbo gave place to Bardot.[1] The women's magazines which before the Second World War had told tales of girls who gave up marriage to become pilots began to run stories about what it was like to be a pilot's wife. Their editors, who had been women, were now men.[2]

It happened even in Russia. In 1924 the Comintern was determined to abolish the family, but as the war years approached women comrades were being exhorted to resume the use of cosmetics, divorce and abortion were stopped, and medals were being given to heroines of the Soviet Union who had borne sixteen children.

The Churches did not fail to profit. The height of the anti-feminist reaction in the 1950s was of course a period of religious boom. Churchmen criticized working mothers, put on family communion, urged family prayers and family grace before meals, and opposed divorce and abortion. Religion flourished in the neo-Victorian climate, and male supremacy in marriage was as fashionable as large families.

It is all over now. One of the assumptions of that period was that the maternal role in child-rearing was all-important.[3] In the '60s the pendulum swung back, and every kind of deviation or delinquency began to be ascribed to lack of an adequate father. So far as we know, after the first months father and mother are *equally* important, and you cannot argue that women have a particular obligation to spend their lives sitting at home. No one has produced evidence that the children of working mothers suffer. It is not true that anatomy is destiny *for women*, but rather that parenthood imposes great obligations on *both* sexes alike.

But, more important, society can no longer afford to regard

[1] And women were once again described as "kittens" or "birds" (pets), "dollies" or "playmates" (childish toys).

[2] Friedan describes these changes amusingly.

[3] John Bowlby, who wrote *Child Care and the Growth of Love*, was the chief theoretician, and "maternal deprivation" was all the rage. Baby books barely mentioned father.

its women members as existing solely for childbearing. In the days before modern medicine, when most lives were short, children were a form of wealth, and raising enough of them to ensure the continuation of the race might take most of a woman's health and energy, through most of her adult life. Modern medicine has utterly changed the situation: its effect upon the lives of women has been and will continue to be far greater than its effect upon the lives of men. Childbearing is no longer difficult or dangerous, and in a time of population explosion women's reproductive capacity begins to seem more of a threat than an asset to society. In the U.S.A. one-third of women of marriageable age are unmarried, and even those who are married may have forty years of very active life ahead of them after they have raised to school age all the children that society needs of them. Furthermore, in advanced technical societies there are hardly any jobs requiring extremes of physical strength or solitary physical daring: almost all the tasks available can be performed by women quite as well as by men. So there can be little doubt that a large-scale resurgence of feminism is on the way, for which the Churches are unprepared. They are not prepared either to utilize its energies, or even to cope with it theoretically. Militant American feminists see the Church as a principal sponsor of an order of relations between the sexes which they are pledged to destroy.

But now it is time to draw a profit-and-loss account, and to try to reach a verdict.

(i) It remains true that Christianity from the first held as a matter of theological principle that women are equally capable of salvation, have equal access to public worship, and may live in a state of religious dedication. In New Testament times we already hear of widows, virgins and deaconesses. They gradually developed and exercised an active ministry until the Constantinian establishment of the Church, when they slowly changed into the various religious Orders of women. It may be said, however, that these ministries of women merely reflected the social fact of female seclusion: women catechists and the like were needed so that access could be gained to women converts. When infant baptism became the norm they were no longer necessary and disappeared.[1] In spite of its theological principle the Church in general accepted the order of things which it found. Only in the last few years has the Roman Catholic Church at last authorized a marriage rite in which the woman is not "given away" by her father and does not promise obedience to her husband.

How Christianity compares with other great religions is a delicate question. Feminism has now affected all parts of the world and all religions. Even Muslim and Hindu apologists claim that their faiths do not teach the inferiority of women. However, for centuries the Jew in his morning Benedictions has blessed God that he was not made a woman, and segregated her in the synagogue. In Islam, women customarily do not attend public prayers, and Sura IV of the Qu'ran plainly asserts the inferiority of women.[2] A Hindu woman rises before her husband, stands till he has finished eating, and goes to bed after him. And so on. In general, male supremacy has been as near total and universal as makes no difference.

(ii) But Christianity has always recognized the possibility of the religious life for women. The extravagant language in which celibacy used to be praised is now in disrepute. Even Aquinas held that virginity is better than marriage, that marriage without sexual intercourse is holier than marriage with it, and that (according to the popular maxim), "He who loves his own wife too ardently is an adulterer."[3] All this is, no doubt rightly, discredited today. But it did say one thing: it said, contrary to the popular opinion, that in order of grace a woman as such need not exist *solely* to fulfil her reproductive function. If celibacy, and indeed sanctity, is a legitimate and praiseworthy possibility for her, then her spiritual dignity is equal to that of man. No

---

[1] How little place the ministry of women has ever had in the Church may be gauged by the endless discussion of whether a woman may baptize. Finally the Council of Florence said yes, in 1439. The puritans were against it: Hooker's *Works* (ed. Keble) II, pp. 280ff.

[2] In Islam a married woman has always been subject to easy divorce: but I do not urge this point, for in Islam a married woman could keep her property and so had a safeguard which Christian women lacked. Notice though, that women have the vote in Egypt, but are not encouraged to use it: a fair example of merely token emancipation.

[3] *Summa Theologiae*, II (ii), 152; III Supp., 42, art. 4; III Supp., 49, art. 6.

doubt the affirmation was made in a distorted and even ugly way, but something like it has reappeared in a secular form in modern feminism. For some nineteenth-century feminists advocated the general abolition of marriage and even of sexual intercourse, and many were themselves spinsters by choice. Miss Rockefeller says in a modern idiom that "Love between a man and a woman is debilitating and counter-revolutionary", which presumably means that for some women at least their moral and spiritual fulfilment demands celibacy. A woman *can* go her own way, like the heroine of *A Doll's House*, and the fact that *some* women can do so says something about all women. In a coarse comparison Freud claimed that it is a woman's deepest desire to be mastered, as it is the deepest desire of a people to be ruled.[1] To assert the possibility of a religious life for women is to deny this, and in fact one of the earliest forms which the feminist movement took in England was the revival of sister-hoods. The Oxford Movement, a highly conservative movement, drew out of the heart of the Christian tradition ideals and principles with which to attack the popular antifeminism of the day. The sisterhoods no doubt worked under male supervision, and kept a strict rule. But at least the tractarians maintained, with the Christian tradition behind them, that the domestic life was not the *only* possible option for women.[2]

(iii) It is also to the credit of the Christian tradition that it has always maintained that the sexes are for each other. Genesis has always been there. Marriage has always been recognized as a holy state of life, even if very grudgingly in certain periods. The extreme misogyny of a Schopenhauer, the extreme misandry (I have had to invent a new word, which is surely a remarkable fact) of Valerie Solanas, have alike been avoided. Christianity is not, like Buddhism, a religion for male celibates, even if the basic texts contain some deplorable statements.[3] This is true even of St. Augustine. However sick-minded he often is when talking about women and about sexuality as they now are, he never

[1] Cited in Rieff, p. 185.
[2] A. M. Allchin, *The Silent Rebellion* (1958). Note, however, T. T. Carter (on p. 78), being careful not to "disparage domestic life by ... comparison" with virginity.
[3] E.g. Revelation 14: 4.

quite forgets that the sexual differentiation of humanity, as originally created by God, was lovely. The theological speculations about human life in paradise in which the old writers abound often seem frivolous. But at least in a man like Augustine, they were a valuable check upon his more savage moods.[1] They preserved a contrast between the relations of the sexes as they now are, and as they ideally might be, upon which the future could build. Memories of paradisal innocence made possible the feminist dreams of later centuries.[2]

Something can also be said here in exculpation of the attitude of English churchmen to relaxation of the divorce laws. By and large, feminists have wanted divorce law reform, and churchmen have opposed it. They did so because for many centuries strict marriage and divorce laws had seemed the right way to protect the position of women: it was here that Christianity was superior to Judaism and Islam. By the 1857 Matrimonial Causes Act, divorce was made possible, but on unequal terms. The husband had only to prove adultery, but a wife petitioning had to prove adultery *plus* cruelty, or desertion for two years. In 1909 a Royal Commission was set up. In its report it proposed an increase in the number of causes of divorce *and* the equality of the sexes in causes of divorce. A minority of three, headed by the Archbishop of York, dissented. But they did *not* dissent on the equality principle, which was duly embodied in the 1923 Matrimonial Causes Act.[3] In general, where churchmen have opposed divorce law reform (or contraception) if they have been wrong their sin was of ignorance, not malice: they believed they were safeguarding the position of women, but their thinking had failed to keep pace with social changes. To say this, however, is not to excuse those who opposed the various Married Women's Property Bills as "an assault upon the sanctity of Christian marriage".[4]

[1] Only a partial check, though. The earlier Augustine held that there would have been no coition in Paradise: later he changed his mind, but he thought that Paradisal coition and parturition would have been so composed and tranquil as not to destroy the woman's virginity!

[2] As the memory of the women of Sparta survived the centuries in which bodily exercises were forbidden to women.

[3] See Ethel Snowden, *The Feminist Movement* (n.d.—c. 1924), pp. 228ff.

[4] Amusing account in E. S. Turner, *Roads to Ruin* (1950), Chapter 6.

(iv) Allowance should also be made for the extent to which male supremacy was reinforced by biological ignorance. The mammalian ovum was first clearly observed and recognized for what it was only in 1827. In 1879 the penetration of a starfish egg by a spermatozoon was observed. But it was only in the present century, with the rise of modern genetics, that it was finally shown that the male and female gametes make a precisely equivalent contribution to determining the character of the offspring (with the exception, of course, of the determination of the offspring's sex, and a few sex-linked characteristics).

It is very difficult now to realize imaginatively the quite different opinions which prevailed in the past. They were of course very varied: but though they seemed to fit the phenomena they also both reflected and reinforced male supremacy.

The agricultural language in which generation is described has in many periods suggested that the male sows his seed in the female, who is like a plot of soil. The male begets *upon* the female: in the language of horse-breeding, the offspring is *by* the sire, *out of* the dam. The male is active, the female passive: he creates, she merely tends and nourishes what he has made. The children are *his*, they bear his name to this day.

This theory was widespread in antiquity,[1] and even in the seventeenth century microscopists were drawing spermatozoa with homunculi (miniature, fully-formed men) sealed up inside. Since these homunculi had the next generation already preformed inside *their* testes and so on we gain a new light on the doctrine of Original Sin. We *were* in Adam. For Aquinas, only the fact that he *had* no human father, and that the mother's contribution is unimportant, saved Christ from the reproach of having paid tithes to Melchizedek while in the loins of Abraham. Original Sin, says Aquinas, is transmitted in the male line.[2] Once it became clear that the female really *does* contribute something Aquinas' own verdict had to be reversed, and the dogma of the Immaculate Conception of Mary was proclaimed to save Christ from inheriting Original Sin through his mother.

---

[1] See the references to Anaxagoras and Aeschylus in Aristotle, 763b and note 3.
[2] *Summa Theologiae*, III, 31, art. 8. For Levi in Abraham's loins see Hebrews 7: 9, 10.

Aristotle's opinions, which Aquinas in the main adopted, were less extreme.[1] They were based on his analysis of a material body into form and matter. A baby is made of two elements, matter and soul. The mother (*mater*, matter) supplies the raw material, nine menstrual discharges of blood saved up. The father contributes soul, nothing material but an active organizing principle, a moving cause. The female, a formless, rounded, sloppy creature, close to earth, and water, lacks the power to do this. Femaleness is incapacity to "concoct" blood; lack of soul-power. Every menstruation is a kind of minor abortion, a proof of woman's inability to form blood into a baby on her own. Hence, "the curse". Now effects resemble causes; if all goes as it should the male will beget upon the female a son who resembles himself. But to do this, he must master his female and impose his form upon her matter: if his vitality is low she will defeat him and he will get a plump shapeless daughter instead of a bony son.[2] Men are hot, women are cold; men are dry, women are moist; the right hand side of the body is hotter, and so more likely to beget a male. Everyone knows that warm-blooded animals are more perfect than cold-blooded; that the right hand is more agile and male, and the left more uncoordinated and female.

Since the father contributes nothing material, Aristotle's biology fits very well with the Logos-flesh Christology of early Christianity. The Logos does just the same job, in the same way, as semen. Aristotle thought parthenogenesis quite possible, and since for Aquinas it is God who creates and puts in the human rational soul at quickening, for him there is not really very much difference between a virginal conception and a normal one. All Aquinas has to do is bridge the gap between conception and quickening, and he does this by bringing the latter forward: unlike us, Christ was a fully-formed human being, with a rational soul in a state of beatitude, upon the instant of his conception.[3]

The mistaken biology of Aristotle, then, decisively influenced many important Christian doctrines, and it helped to make

[1] For what follows, see *The Generation of Animals, passim.*
[2] See also Lucretius, *De Rerum Natura*, IV.
[3] *Summa Theologiae*, III, 33.

the primacy of the male sex so obvious as to remain unquestioned till the Renaissance.

(v) But more than this, even my cursory description shows that the way Aristotle—and everybody else before modern times—thought of male and female is an integral part of an entire world-view. We can set it out in parallel columns:

male	female
active	passive
form	matter
right	left
air/fire	water/earth
hot/dry	moist/cold
sky	earth
above	below
hard	soft
angular	rounded
independent	dependent
strong	weak
stable	volatile/fickle

In short, the way Aristotle conceived the relation of the sexes was his entire cosmology in miniature. And if God surpasses the world as the male surpasses the female, then it is fitting to speak of God in male imagery.

And this at last tells us the true reason for the rise of feminism: it is a by-product of secularization.[1] Only when mankind's ancient ways of thinking were overthrown was it possible to demythologize woman and challenge male primacy.

This explains Mill's remark that the continuing subjection of women in his time was an extraordinary anachronism: "a single relic of an old world of thought and practice exploded in everything else but retained in the one thing of most universal interest."[2]

(vi) Finally, Christianity has shared a common European assumption that women, unlike men, cannot satisfactorily reconcile sex and intellect, marriage and career. The biological demand that she fulfil her reproductive role is seen as threatening

---

[1] For other explanations see O'Neill, 15ff.
[2] Mill, 237.

her spiritual freedom. For Freud, in *men*, intellect can govern sexuality; but, in *women*, must submit to it. De Beauvoir, under the proximate influence of Sartre and the remote influence of Descartes, sees the long cycle of conception, pregnancy, parturition and suckling as an alienating and somehow diminishing experience. The woman's psyche is invaded and drowned by the vast impersonal force of the species. Similarly, in Catholicism, there is a tiny minority of married women saints, but their *legenda* with striking regularity associate the beginning of their sanctity with their first attempts to discontinue marital relations with their husbands.[1] Feminists and anti-feminists have shared the assumption that the fulfilment of woman's reproductive function is inimical to her spiritual freedom and must bring her under male domination. Generations of feminists, both Christian and post-Christian, have therefore seen it as necessary to reject marriage. The moral good that Christianity has done by idealizing the figure of the Madonna and Child has thus been partly undermined.

In conclusion, Christianity, adopting a mythical world-picture, in effect taught the inferiority of women until the present century. Even Karl Barth, the best-known theologian of this century, still taught male primacy.[2] But, once stated, the feminist case is irresistible, and has now affected even Muslim countries. Christianity can fairly claim that it always carried latent within it the principle of the equal moral dignity of the sexes. But it will be unable to make the necessary changes in attitude without a very considerable effort to throw off the past: for in any culture the way the relation of the sexes is conceived reflects in a profound manner an entire world-view.

[1] Blessed Angela of Foligno is the most extreme example. She prayed for and obtained the deaths of her entire family.
[2] *Church Dogmatics*, III, 4: Bailey, 293f.

4

IS MONOTHEISM ESSENTIALLY
INTOLERANT?

DOES CHRISTIAN belief make for intolerance? Bertrand Russell thought so. A lecture he gave in 1927, entitled "Why I am not a Christian", has lately been reprinted again. In it he claimed that Christians have "for the most part" been "extremely wicked". "The more intense has been the religion of any period, and the more profound has been the dogmatic belief, the greater has been the cruelty and the worse has been the state of affairs. In the so-called ages of faith, when men really did believe the Christian religion . . . there was the Inquisition"— and the burning of witches. The Churches, says Russell, have consistently been the enemies of progress in human feeling and in the diminution of misery. Why? Because religion is based upon fear, and "fear is the parent of cruelty, and therefore it is no wonder that religion and cruelty have gone hand in hand".[1]

Whether or not religion is based upon fear we shall decide later, but certainly Christianity arose in an atmosphere of bitter controversy. The New Testament period found Jew set against Gentile, Jew against Samaritan, Pharisee against Sadducee: and then came the Christians to make matters worse. Christian is set against Jew, and Jewish Christian against Greek Christian: orthodox Christian disputes with gnostic Christian, Christian denounces pagan idolater—it was a ferociously quarrelsome time. Both in St. Paul and in the Gospels we see an odd inconsistency. There is an ethic of love, of mutual forbearance, of forgiveness; but, coexisting with it, vehement denunciations of doctrinal enemies. Like, perhaps, some other great religions, Christianity was born in faction, strife,

[1] *Why I am not a Christian* (1957 edn.), pp. 14–16.

69

disputation. Love of the brethren went with detestation of those outside the brotherhood. Finally, as Church and Synagogue drew apart, they settled down contentedly to centuries of mutual character assassination.

The violence and folly of religious disputes has made them a byword. In Ulster now they are marching and counter-marching, sublimely oblivious of anything but their own conviction that they are right. Each "we" defines itself by opposition to a "they": in us is all virtue, in them all evil; and it is hard to say whether we hate them because we love each other, or love each other because we hate them.[1] It is not surprising that sensible politicians try to damp down religious passions. Jonathan Swift, who loved Ireland, said once that "We have just enough Religion to make us hate, but not enough to make us love one another";[2] but most people would doubt whether *more* of the sort of religion there is in Northern Ireland would make for peace. For it is precisely religion which has kept Ulster trapped in the past, poor and politically backward. Indeed there is rather a widespread belief nowadays that the more religious a man is, the more biased his judgement, and the less fitted he is for the conduct of public affairs. J. F. Kennedy, campaigning for the United States Presidency a decade ago, had to assure the American people that he would not allow the fact that he was a Catholic to influence his judgement, or make him less impartial in conducting that office.[3] If a British Member of Parliament says that he is distressed by some of the consequences of our present rather lax abortion law, his opponents will point to the fact that he is a Catholic as evidence that his moral judgement is not disinterested and should not be seriously regarded. There is a fallacy in this, the popular modern fallacy that moral judgement can be made by "research" alone, by a systematic gathering and impartial scrutiny of the facts and nothing else: but leaving aside that fallacy, there still remains the popular connexion of religion with bias or prejudice. If people hold to an opinion on abortion

[1] On "we" and "they", see some suggestive remarks in Richard Hughes' novel, *The Fox in the Attic* (1961), Chapter 26.

[2] *Thoughts on Various Subjects*, 1.

[3] People sometimes criticize St. Luke for labouring to show Rome that Christianity was politically innocuous; but the same manœuvre is common today.

on what are called "religious grounds" it is customary to pay a formal tribute to their sincerity, but not to their rationality: which amounts to saying that "religious grounds" are not grounds at all, but mere prejudice.

Bertrand Russell's claim that Christianity, on the record, has been cruel and reactionary, raises many and complex questions; questions which do not relate solely to the period between Constantine and the French Revolution. Some of these questions are easier to answer than others. There are, I think, three main types of question: (a) straightforward historical questions; (b) questions about group responsibility; and (c) questions about the inner nature of a religion, the kind of man and of actions it tends to produce. We will take an example of each in turn.

(a) We may ask a straightforward historical question such as "Is it true that Christian Churches have in the past practised and encouraged the punishment of people for holding unauthorized religious opinions?" Or we may ask "Did the Church in the past impose on its members a strict moral discipline enforced by penal sanctions applied by special Church courts?" Questions like these can be settled. The answer is in the affirmative. Larger questions of interpretation like "Just how bad is the Church's record in respect of anti-semitism?" are controversial and difficult to handle impartially. One must be careful in the selection and deployment of evidence. But there is no disputing the decrees on the Jews of the Fourth Lateran Council of 1215: and there is no disputing that they *are* a piece of evidence of the first importance.

(b) A question like "How far is the Roman Catholic Church to blame for the Spanish Inquisition?" is more delicate. We need to be clear about the sense in which a group can be called a moral agent, and about what actions count as evidence in the making of moral judgements about a group. Fortunately a group like the Roman Catholic Church, in which authority is highly centralized, is relatively easy to pronounce upon. One knows fairly well which pronouncements are official pronouncements, which policies and actions are official policies and actions. With other groups this may not be so. Furthermore, in discussing such questions one must beware of the notion of hereditary guilt. Sometimes a freethinker who would reject any notion of inherited sinfulness as immoral will inconsistently blame the present-day Church for what it used to be. He can only justly do this insofar as he can show that old policies have not been abandoned, but only shelved for a while; or that the evil consequences of bad old policies still live on, or something of the kind.

Still, the question of blame for the Spanish Inquisition is discussible. It is arguable that it was an organ of the State rather than of the Church, and that some Popes made efforts to check its worst excesses. But the idea had been the Church's in the first place: Innocent III founded the Holy Office at Rome in 1208. And for centuries the Church had been delivering culprits to the civil arm for punishment.[1] It always accompanied this action with a plea that he be mercifully treated—that is, not killed or maimed. But Boniface VIII said that the Church should still hand a man over even though it were certain that its plea would not be heard. And the Church sentenced to death. What is more, the magistrate eventually became liable to excommunication if he varied the sentence, or failed to carry it out within six days, so that the plea for mercy became purely formal, like the rule that the clergy were not to shed blood.

The Inquisition was, of course, staffed by clergy, and even had its theologians, such as the egregious Paramo, who wrote a book *On the Origin and Progress of the Holy Office of the Inquisition* (Madrid 1598).[2] Paramo called God the First Inquisitor, and the first hearing and sentence that upon Adam and Eve. He finds in the Genesis story a model of the Inquisition's procedure. Divine judgement works itself out in human history: its aim is always to purge and heal the social body. Now God has delegated to his Church the power to bind and loose, to execute judgement on his behalf. The Church is God's instrument, and the Holy Office its principal tool. A theology of history must give central place to the work of the Inquisition.

Now Paramo's work is nothing freakish: it has a thousand years of history behind it. The first time capital punishment for

[1] On these topics see J. Lecler, *Toleration and the Reformation* (ET, 1960).
[2] An account of Paramo in Mandell Creighton, *Persecution and Tolerance* (1895).

72

heresy was instigated by the Church is said to be the case of Priscillian and some of his followers in 385. It is often pointed out that St. Martin and St. Ambrose protested against it, and so they did: but St. Martin was a well-known smasher of pagan temples, and St. Ambrose approved the burning of a synagogue.[1] What they disapproved of was not persecution as such, but that the Church should have procured executions. Still, at the end of the fourth century a certain escalation did undoubtedly take place, and it was particularly St. Augustine who made a reluctant but substantial contribution to the theory and practice of persecution.

Difficult though it may be to decide how far a body is to be blamed for the acts of some of its members, there is no doubt that the theory and practice of persecution is deeply embedded in the history of the Church, in the practice of its central government as much as in its outworks. Loudly though the Reformers demanded liberty for their own opinions, they took over the practice of persecution almost unquestioningly, and Paramo himself could not equal the ferocity of the book Calvin wrote to justify the burning of Servetus.[2]

In 1965 the Declaration on Religious Freedom (*Dignitatis Humanae Personae*) was promulgated by the Second Vatican Council. The American Jesuit, John Courtney Murray, who was influential in its framing, comments that "The course of the development between the *Syllabus of Errors* (1864) and . . . (1965) . . . still remains to be explained by theologians."[3] No doubt it will be. But we should not be surprised if people suspect that this conversion has come rather late and with little enthusiasm. The text of the Declaration avoids any express repudiation of past errors and confines itself to saying rather circuitously that in the course of Church history "there have at times appeared ways of acting which were less in accord with the spirit of the gospel and even opposed to it. Nevertheless the doctrine of the Church that no one is to be coerced into faith has always stood firm." But not even this last statement can be accepted without qualification:

---

[1] *Letter XI*, to the Emperor Theodosius.
[2] *Declaration pour Maintenir la Vraye Foi* (1554).
[3] *Documents of Vatican II*, ed. W. M. Abbott (1967), p. 673.

the Church's teaching is best represented by St. Thomas Aquinas, who did indeed hold that faith is a voluntary act. Jews and pagans ought not to be compelled to the Faith, though force should be used if possible to prevent them from hindering the true faith. But Aquinas holds that force may and should be used to compel heretics and apostates to return to the true Faith, because they put themselves irrevocably under the Church's jurisdiction when they underwent baptism.[1] In fact the classical Catholic teaching was that persecution was to be used not to extend the Church, but rather to maintain it. In pursuit of this latter end almost anything was justifiable. Calvinists, by contrast, tended to persecute, not in this rather pragmatic spirit, but out of zeal for God's honour.

In sum, the question of whether the Church is to blame for the Spanish Inquisition is at least discussible. We can and do make moral judgements about institutions. Such judgements need to be based on the official policy and actions of the institution observed over a sufficient period. In respect of persecution we can produce abundant evidence of this kind. In so far as the mentality which persecuted still survives, it makes sense still to blame. This is *not* to admit notions of hereditary guilt, but only to say that where the Church does still have power it does still use it in ways recognizably of a piece with the bad old practices. Progressive theologians may be harassed, small Protestant minority groups may be chased a little, a discreet censorship over literature and the arts may continue, inequitable regulations may still be in force in respect of marriages between Catholics and non-Catholics, and dissenting priests may be suspended from the ministry of the word and/or the sacraments without proper trial or right of appeal. Insofar as such practices continue, and the past has still not been clearly disowned, blame may still be justly attributed.

(c) A still more difficult type of question is this: the Church was born of faction. From the first it included and excluded; there was always a procedure for expelling people from membership. Now, was an intolerant and persecuting spirit part of Christianity from the first, bound up with its theology: or was its

[1] *Summa Theologiae*, II (ii), 10, art. 8.

74

connexion with Christianity accidental, belonging to a particular historical epoch now happily ended?

This is a question about the theology and the inner spirit of a religion; how it works out in practice, what kind of man it tends to produce. It is a complex question, and both the attack and the defence have many possible moves to make.

One important line of defence must be cleared out of the way at the outset. It is the *relativist defence,* and it argues as follows: up to the seventeenth century it was held almost universally that social cohesion largely depended upon religious uniformity. The state was a relatively fragile structure, and it needed to be held together by religion. In antiquity they distinguished, not between natural theology and revelation, but between natural theology and *civil* theology. If a magnate founded a new city, he would hire a theologian to devise a cult for it. When the new city of Alexandria was built, Ptolemy I appointed a *Kultusminister,* Timotheus, who in collaboration with an Egyptian priest named Manetho simply invented the cult of Serapis.[1] In spite of the execution of Socrates, Plato, when drawing up plans for ideal cities, did not hesitate to outline their religions (the "Noble Lie") and even (in the *Laws*) to propose a system of persecution to ensure that the cult was piously observed.[2] So it may be argued that moderns, who are accustomed to religious pluralism within a secular state, must allow for the quite different assumptions of the past. Until the seventeenth century nobody really could be sure that a secular state would stand: religious persecution was universally regarded as a regrettable political necessity.

But there are certain objections to this relativist defence. In the first place it may be argued that there were nevertheless always *some* people who disapproved of religious persecution and the way in which, in antiquity, religion and politics were interwoven. Some people could see that persecution was wrong, so why could they not persuade the others? Why does it have to be the case that the zealous persecutor is always remembered as more orthodox, more characteristically Christian, than his liberal opponent, so that Calvin seems more orthodox than

---

[1] See Benjamin Farrington, *The Faith of Epicurus* (1967), Chapters 6 and 7.
[2] Book X.

Castellio, Luther than Erasmus, St. Bernard than Abelard? There always were *some* liberals. Epicurus rebelled against Plato. In any case it is arguable that the Roman Empire was more tolerant of religious diversity *before* the establishment of Christianity than *after*.

In the second place, the relativist defence greatly diminishes the moral authority of the past, in which Christianity has usually been thought to have an interest. Take the case of anti-semitism: hideously anti-semitic utterances in plenty emanated from Christians as diverse as John Chrysostom and Luther.[1] Now if contemporaries of our own used the language of Luther about Jews, we should think so badly of what they said that we should have very little esteem for their opinions on any other matter of religion or morals. Why then do we continue to give high moral authority to men in the past who said such things? If we try to exculpate them by some form of the relativist defence we cannot but relativize their opinions on other matters as well. They cease to have any real authority for us. If you admit that Luther said many horrible things, but you deny that moral judgements are historically relative to the time in which they are made, your only recourse is to rewrite Church history, making the heroes not Bernard, Luther and Calvin, but Abelard, Erasmus and Castellio. Like the left-wing radicals in the Reformation, you will be driven to try to discern a new succession of good men and true in the record, a different succession from that hitherto accepted in the Church.

So the relativist defence cannot accomplish very much: the authority of the past, or at any rate of the Church's traditional picture of its own past, will be greatly diminished whatever you do.

Another line of attack and defence can be discerned in Mandell Creighton's reply to W. E. H. Lecky.

Lecky, one of the ablest of a long line of rationalist historians, published in 1865 a *History of the Rise and Influence of the Spirit of Rationalism in Europe*. This book offers a classical theory of how the Christian Church became intolerant and persecuting. Briefly it argues that Christianity makes an over-

---

[1] See the evidence in Malcolm Hay, *The Foot of Pride* (later reissued as *Europe and the Jews*), 1950.

whelming claim on its adherents. If membership of the Church is the indispensable condition for attaining eternal salvation, almost anything is justified in order to get people into the Church and keep them there. Transitory suffering, temporal pain, is nothing compared with a man's eternal destiny. So when the Church gained power, it naturally persecuted.

Now apologists for persecution certainly have often produced theological justifications for what they were doing. For example, Pope Innocent III argued that since God punishes children for the sins of their fathers the Church may do the same, and by confiscating the goods of heretics reduce their children to want.[1] Paramo reckoned that the work of the Spanish Inquisition was God's work, done by the Church in God's way. Arguments of this kind strongly suggest that Christians became cruel men because they believed in a cruel God.

Eighteenth-century sceptics had run very close to saying this in so many words. The best example was David Hume, in his book *The Natural History of Religion* (1757).[2] Hume connected "the narrow implacable spirit of the Jews"[3] with their monotheism. Polytheism was relatively indulgent, but monotheism is almost inevitably intolerant. Where there is but one God, one revelation, one standard of truth and goodness, one proper form of worship, all else is impiety and a fit object of both divine and human vengeance.[4] God's infinite superiority to mankind "is apt, when joined with superstitious terrors, to sink the human mind into the lowest submission and abasement, and to represent the monkish virtues of mortification, penance, humility, and passive suffering, as the only qualities which are acceptable to him".[5] To satisfy such a temperament, theology must become elaborate, authoritative and mysterious, so that rebellious reason may be subdued "by the belief of the most unintelligible sophisms".[6] A grotesque contradiction arises: "our natural terrors present the notion of a devilish and

[1] Lecky, Volume II, p. 36n.
[2] Citations from the edition by H. E. Root (1956).
[3] p. 50.
[4] p. 49.
[5] p. 52.
[6] p. 54.

malicious deity: Our propensity to adulation leads us to acknowledge an excellent and divine."[1] Ecstatic applause must be given to a character which a cool judgement would think abominable. There can be no doubt that Hume's early exposure to the preaching of "predestinarian doctors" helped shape his opinions on the psychology of religion,[2] and show him why some of the most zealous men of faith have been not only deeply divided personalities but also vigorous persecutors.

Edward Gibbon's opinions run close to Hume. He too mentions "the sullen obstinacy of the Jews" and gives this portrait of their God under cover of expounding Gnosticism: "A being liable to passion and to error, capricious in his favour, implacable in his resentment, meanly jealous of his superstitious worship, and confining his partial providence to a single people and to this transitory life."[3] We might compare this with Winwood Reade: "While the other potentates of the celestial world lived in harmony together, Jehovah was a sullen and solitary being, who separated his people from the rest of mankind, forbade them to eat and drink with those who were not of their own race, and threatened to punish them if they worshipped any gods but him": belief in such a God "engenders a slavish and oriental condition of mind".[4]

We might dismiss such remarks as foolish and prejudiced: but moral objection to the character of God and of the righteous believer as they are portrayed in parts of the Old Testament has a long history. For example, Dr. Moira Dearnley has summarized eighteenth-century criticism of the pre-Christian morality of the Psalms:[5] and no very satisfactory reply to such criticism has been given by theologians. And the themes which we have already noticed in Hume are substantially the same as those taken up by Nietzsche in *The Genealogy of Morals* (1887), and in later, crazier books such as *Twilight of the Idols* (1888) and still more *The Antichrist* of the same year. Nietzsche of course

---

[1] Citations from the edition by H. E. Root (1956), p. 66.
[2] See p. 68n.
[3] *Decline and Fall of the Roman Empire* (1776–88), Chapter XV.
[4] *The Martyrdom of Man* (1872), cited from the 15th edn., (1896), pp. 482, 543.
[5] *Theology*, vol. LXXIII, No. 598 (April 1970), pp. 161ff. See also T. R. Henn, *The Bible as Literature* (1970), Chapter 12.

admired the vigorous early Old Testament faith: but his characterization of Christian psychology is in line with Hume. Nietzsche's "slave morality" corresponds to Hume's "monkish virtues": both see in classical Christian otherworldliness a kind of spiritual sickness, a self-hatred; but Nietzsche, with his vastly superior psychological insight, can trace more clearly the way in which an ethic of self-punishment leads to resentment and cruelty.

Now it is true that some theologians have run very close to believing, and admitting they believed, in a cruel God. For example, Erasmus objected to Luther that a stiff doctrine of predestination made God seem odious and human effort worthless. "Who will believe that God loves him?" Luther: "I reply, Nobody! Nobody can! But the elect shall believe it, and the rest shall perish without believing it." Faith's object is hidden, hidden under a contrary appearance. "Thus when God quickens, He does so by killing; when he justifies, he does so by pronouncing guilty; when he carries up to heaven, he does so by bringing down to hell." He hides his mercy behind wrath, his righteousness beneath unrighteousness. "The highest degree of faith is to believe that he is merciful, though he saves so few and damns so many, though of his own will he makes us perforce proper subjects for damnation ... the impossibility of understanding makes room for the exercise of faith."[1] In short, God predestines some to think him cruel (as indeed to commonsense he appears to be), sends them to hell, and there confirms their belief: others he predestines to believe that in spite of appearances he is nevertheless merciful; these he sends to heaven and there confirms *their* belief. Whether he is *really* cruel or kind seems hardly a meaningful question, for there is no impartial standpoint from which it can be raised. The human will is "a beast standing between two riders ... If God rides it, it wills and goes where God wills ... If Satan rides, it wills and goes where Satan wills. Nor may it choose to which rider it will run, or which it will seek, but the riders themselves fight to decide who shall have and hold it."[2]

---

[1] *De Servo Arbitrio*, 1525 (*The Bondage of the Will*, tr. J. I. Packer and O. R. Johnston 1957), pp. 99–101.
[2] *ibid.*, pp. 103f.

One might wish to say straight away that theologies which teach arbitrary election, the damnation of unbaptized infants and the like are obviously morally odious. But the matter is not quite so simple. Men used to say that behind a frowning providence God hid a smiling face; they insisted that God's immediate aspect might well appear capricious and cruel, but that in the end right would prevail; and this harsh theology helped them to face the hardships of life with fortitude.

In modern times too many men have been seduced into believing that all human woes can be removed by the application of "research", good will and money. Over the scene presides a God who is a nebulous, stylized benignity. We are very ill-equipped to cope with evil, because the popular modern theology gives us no way of coping with it. God is either purely loving, or non-existent. By contrast, the harsh dramatic theologies of the past gave a pilgrim people courage to face life's adversities, and continue steadfastly believing that they would come through. If one judges a theology on utilitarian grounds there is something to be said for the old cruel doctrines. They produced immense strength of character when life was often cruel, ironically cruel, as it still is. But did they make men *more* cruel? Lecky argued that the savage theologies of the period between, let us say, Augustine and Chillingworth, hardened men's hearts.[1] Before their eyes was thrust constantly the spectacle of suffering, often undeserved. The twisted body of the Crucified, the pains of purgatory, the damnation of unbaptized infants, the long parade of martyrs and confessors, the self-punishment of ascetics, the awful anger of God, the persecution of Jews and heretics. And "not only were men constantly expatiating on these ghastly pictures, they were constantly associating them with gladness and joy".[2] Suffering became a positive good to be sought; and Julian of Norwich prayed for it.[3] A long line of free-thinkers has passed down from hand to hand for quotation the texts from Tertullian,[4]

---

[1] Lecky, Chapters III and IV, Part One.
[2] *ibid.*, Vol. i, p. 321, and the following pages.
[3] *Revelations of Divine Love* (after 1373), Chapter 2.
[4] *De Spectaculis*, XXX.

Aquinas,[1] and Dante,[2] which describe the satisfaction of the blessed in contemplating the torments of the damned.

To be fair we have to consider a complex equation. A harsh theology may suit a harsh time. It is easy for us now to forget what life was like before modern medicine, modern technology, and modern social administration—what it was like, at least, for nineteen people out of twenty. A harsh theology may develop fortitude, and enable people to cope with evil. But it may also make people still crueller. The same forces by which it binds the Christian folk together in mutual love may make them hate those who betray the folk, or are outside it, still more. Philadelphia may prompt xenophobia. If one of the purposes of a theology is to bind a people together, then the love among *us* is purchased, or often purchased, at the price of hatred of *them*. In harsh times, which produce apocalyptic theologies, the line between *us* and *them* becomes an unbridgeable gulf; the love and the hatred alike are screwed up to the very highest pitch. In easier times one can afford to be laxer and more benign, but Christianity was born in apocalyptic times and has never quite shaken off the influence of those days. In the recorded teaching of Jesus the mild and liberal ethic of reciprocal love and humility coexists with the denunciations of the Pharisees and threats of hell-fire. Whether both these elements go back to Jesus himself may be a matter for dispute: but they certainly go back to the earliest Church. For example, threats of divine retribution against "the Jews" who rejected Christ are built into the New Testament documents.[3]

To return at last to our question: Russell said that "religion and cruelty go hand in hand", a metaphor which may suggest that perhaps there was a time before they joined hands, and that there will come a time when they will separate for good. Lecky, however, held that intolerance and a spirit of persecution were built in from the first, and follow from the character of Christianity as an apocalyptic religion of salvation by faith.

---

[1] *Summa Theologiae*, III, Supp., 93, 94.

[2] *Inferno*, VIII, 31ff; XXXII, 70ff. Dante abuses and kicks the damned.

[3] See H. J. Schoeps, *The Jewish-Christian Argument* (ET 1965), especially Chapter III.

To this charge Mandell Creighton attempted a reply in a course of Hulsean Lectures delivered here in the year 1893–94.[1] His conclusions were:

(1) that persecution, or the infliction of punishment for erroneous opinions, was contrary to the express teaching of Christ, and was alien to the spirit of Christianity; (2) was adopted by the Church from the system of the world, when the Church accepted the responsibility of maintaining order in the community; (3) was really exercised for political rather than religious ends; (4) was always condemned by the Christian conscience; (5) was felt by those who used it to land them in contradictions; (6) neither originated in any misunderstanding of the Scriptures nor was removed by the progress of intellectual enlightenment, but (7) disappeared because the State became conscious that there was an adequate basis for the maintenance of political society in those principles of right and wrong which were universally recognised by its citizens, apart from their position or beliefs as members of any religious organisation.[2]

In short, Creighton regarded persecution as a phenomenon of the Christendom era, now over. The Church had allowed itself to be exploited by the State, and Creighton fully admitted the horrors of that period. Why had it ended? Not because secular reason had finally triumphed over superstition and broken the power of the Church, but rather because the true spirit of Christianity had reasserted itself within the Church, through the long debates on religious liberty which began, however uncertainly, at the Reformation. "Those prejudices which are the legacy of the days of persecution"[3] still exist, Creighton admits, and he is cautious enough to warn that late nineteenth-century toleration is a "tender plant and needs jealous watching"; but on the whole he is optimistic.

We have already suggested some reasons for doubting whether Creighton's arguments are strong enough. He confines himself to persecution in the sense of the infliction of some kind

---

[1] *Persecution and Tolerance* (1895).
[2] pp. 2f.
[3] p. 139.

of physical punishment for the holding of unauthorized (Creighton says "erroneous", which begs the question) opinions as such. He detaches persecution, in this rather narrow sense, from its context. He *assumes* the context, and it is the context which is important. By the context I mean such statements as these: that Christianity is a strongly *doctrinal* religion; that the Church *knows* which beliefs are true and which erroneous; that the authorities in the Church have the duty to enforce true belief within the Church and expel heretics from membership of the Church; and that vehemence of language in the assault upon heresy is right and proper. But once this context is given, the difference between the way controversies were conducted in the mid-fourth century, and the way they were conducted in the early fifth century, is only a matter of degree. The controversies between the Church and the Synagogue were conducted in such a way that whichever side eventually prevailed and was able to call upon the aid of the civil power would as surely persecute the other as night follows day.[1] When Christianity prevailed, it naturally reduced Judaism to its classical position of historical impotence. Seeking to create a society which bodied forth Christian doctrine, it gave visible expression to the supposed theological truth of the rejection of the Jews by God, by ensuring that the Jews became a wretched, fugitive people. It would be contrary to Christian doctrine if any Jew employed a Christian servant, or indeed if any Jew were ever better off than any Christian. The truth that God had cast off his ancient people was made socially evident. That this should eventually come about followed by stages from the way Christian doctrine was framed at the first.[2]

And Creighton was not cautious enough about the future. Even as he wrote Europe was afire with anti-semitism, from Russia to Portugal. The Dreyfus affair had begun, the Kiev ritual murder trial was to come. The Church was implicated in the revival of anti-semitism. In the twentieth century sharply reactionary forms of Christianity have flourished. Churches have made concordats with such notabilities as Stalin, Hitler

[1] James Parkes, *The Conflict of the Church and the Synagogue* (1934).
[2] Evidence in Hay and Parkes, *op. cit.*

and Franco. Christianity has been as willing as ever to lend itself to secular political movements, often of the most evil kind, such as nationalism and racialism. If Creighton thought that Christianity, in his day, had recovered and would remain true to its own distinctive spirit, he would have been sadly disappointed by Church history since his time.

We have been discussing the question, whether an intolerant and potentially persecuting spirit was part of Christianity from the first, being bound up with its basic beliefs and the way they were held: or whether its association with Christianity was an accident, a deplorable accident of history? We see now how difficult that question is. It is always *possible* to say with Chesterton that "Christianity has not been tried and found wanting. It has not been tried." But that is a rather empty manœuvre, making the definition of what is to count as Christianity something so rarefied that next to nothing in all Church history can be reckoned a true expression of it. If one judges on the record and says that the only sensible way to discover what is Christianity is to look at the whole story of what the Church has claimed and been, then it *does* look rather as if an intolerant and persecuting spirit has been prominent at many or most times and places.

But I cannot agree with Russell that the reason for this is that "religion is based primarily upon fear". It is an old theory, going back before Hume[1] and Hobbes[2] to Epicurus. Nineteenth-century travellers, encountering primitive religion, emphasized the fearfulness of it, and Freud made a famous comparison between religious rituals and the behaviour of obsessional neurotics. But it would be better to compare religious rituals with the culture of childhood, and the elaborate rules of games devised both by children and adults. Modern anthropologists would repudiate any such generalization as "Religion is based upon fear".[3]

Nor to my mind is there much plausibility in attempts to define the religious man as a distinctive psychological type. A

[1] *Natural History*, pp. 26ff.
[2] *Leviathan* (1651), Part 1, Chapter 12.
[3] E.g. Mary Douglas, *Purity and Danger* (1966), Introduction.

great deal of this has been done, by Nietzsche, Freud and others. But there is not the slightest reason to suppose that religious people share a common and peculiar psychopathology. The sketching of a psychopathology of religion by Hume, Nietzsche or Freud is usually an amusing polemical move in the moral criticism of religion. It can be done with a good deal of satirical wit. But it should not be mistaken for an empirical hypothesis which could be verified by subjecting the bench of Bishops to a psychological test.

No, the serious points which have arisen from our discussion reduce to two; the peculiarly Christian institution of the *Church* as an exclusive society of those who are to be saved, and the status of *dogma*. Moral criticism of the Church's record of intolerance bears at last upon how the Church thinks of itself and of its belief. But sorting out the case for and against organized religion will take us another chapter.

5

THE BITTER RECORD OF
ORGANIZED RELIGION

BY THE end of the last chapter we reached the brink of a whole series of questions about the way Christianity expresses itself visibly in that strange institution, the Church.

But before plunging into them, we should utter a word of caution. For generations now "organized religion" has been a derogatory phrase. Any fool can hammer the Church, and many do: it is a large and inviting target, and much of the criticism has an air of immaturity about it. One is reminded of an adolescent's criticism of his parents for not living up to unrealistically high standards: an analogy all too apt in the case of Kierkegaard's attack on Bishops Mynster and Martensen.[1] Often the weakness of the criticism is shown by the fact that the charges are contradictory. Contradictory accusations are a reliable sign of prejudice, for example when new immigrants into a community are accused both of being workshy and of stealing the best jobs.[2] In the same way the Church may be criticized *both* for being "out of touch", *and* for "interfering"; it is attacked if it silently endures an unjust government, and it is attacked if it advocates the overthrow of the régime; it is attacked for being a domineering "establishment" by people who in other contexts revile it as a dwindling, ineffectual minority; it is attacked for being reactionary and yet ridiculed if it becomes progressive; it is attacked for indoctrinating children by the same people who are eager to prove that it fails totally to indoctrinate them.

---

[1] *Kierkegaard's Attack upon Christendom* (tr. Lowrie), 1944.
[2] Kimball Young, *Handbook of Social Psychology* (1957 edn., pp. 555ff.), describes native American hostility to successive waves of immigrants.

Attacks on the Church's wealth often come from people who are not likely themselves ever to be obliged to live within the narrow limits of the income of the average priest. Kierkegaard himself acted on the principle of attacking the best, so it is fair to retort against him that his bitter criticisms of clerical stipends were made by a man who himself lived lavishly on inherited money. It is common to hear people reproach the Church for being out of touch with *them*, but less common to hear people reproach *themselves* for being out of touch with the Church. Nineteenth-century Christianity was outstandingly energetic in all kinds of philanthropic endeavour, and yet in spite of all its labours people persisted with the charge that the Church was concerned only with the next life, and not with this.[1] If a clergyman, eager to refute this latter charge, weighed in with some pronouncement about armaments or economics, he was sure to be told that such matters were not his business!

People have strong feelings about organized religion, and the whole topic is clouded over with bad arguments and prejudice. Perhaps they fall into making contradictory charges because the subject is so difficult to handle. There is no shortage of evidence; rather, a surfeit. Walter Shewring,[2] discussing the question of wealth and poverty, points out that the history of Christian practice in this matter can be presented either favourably or unfavourably. The apologist can produce his line of generous and compassionate souls: the critic can produce "equally continuous evidence of the abuse of riches, social injustice, oppression of the poor". The Church is big and old and varied enough for both to be right in what they affirm. Whether a historian comes down upon one side or the other may depend more upon his prejudices than upon a review of *all* the evidence.

Because the evidence is so abundant, surprisingly discordant verdicts upon organized religion can each be given some appearance of plausibility. At one extreme stands the rationalist who sees in the past a gradual triumph of reason over

[1] W. O. Chadwick, *The Victorian Church*, II (1970), pp. 269ff.
[2] *Rich and Poor in Christian Tradition* (1948), p. 7.

ecclesiastical bigotry and intolerance. Bertrand Russell's statement is typical:

> You find as you look around the world that every single bit of progress in human feeling, every improvement in the criminal law, every step towards the diminution of war, every step towards better treatment of the coloured races, or every mitigation of slavery, every moral progress that there has been in the world, has been consistently opposed by the organized Churches of the world. I say quite deliberately that the Christian religion, as organized in its Churches, has been and still is the principal enemy of moral progress in the world.[1]

Notice that Russell does not deny that individual Christians have been good men. The typical situation he has in mind is one where individuals may oppose a war, or oppose slavery, but the weight of the institutional Church as such is thrown on the other side. His emphasis is not upon Christianity, but upon the Christian religion as organized in its Churches. He could admit Shewring's point about the diversity of the evidence, but still claims that while individual Christians may give away their wealth, Churches never do.

At the opposite extreme stand those who use the *Moral Capital Argument* and the notorious *Roman Empire Argument*. The former is used by many respectable conservatives, and even a heretic's heretic like Walter Kaufmann concedes that (though unsound) it is "perhaps the best defense of organized religion".[2] The argument is that as a matter of fact the Church has been the principal witness to and transmitter of the moral ideals of our culture. To weaken the Church is to weaken the moral fabric of society because, apart from a handful of inner-directed intellectuals who believe in "the autonomy of ethics", the mass of men as a matter of fact ultimately owe their moral principles to religious authority. Standards of justice and respect for individuals, ideals of mercy and disinterested love depend for their maintenance upon the efforts of organized religion, which as a matter of fact is the moral spine of society. The freethinker who rejects organized religion lives

[1] *Why I am not a Christian* (1957), p. 15.
[2] *The Faith of a Heretic* (1961), §69: Anchor edn. (1963), p. 268.

on Christian moral capital, which, experience shows, is dissipated in a generation or two. Trace with Lord Annan[1] the biographies of the intelligentsia: great-grandfather was a Clapham Sect evangelical; grandfather a strenuous agnostic; father an aesthete; and son's career is too lamentable to record in detail. No, whether or not Christianity is true, and whatever the logical merits of the autonomy of ethics, the wise man who has a sense of social reality will join the agnostic schoolmaster who believes in compulsory Chapel, because organized religion is necessary to bind a society together.

This is the classic Ciceronian defence of organized religion:[2] a little further to the right we have the *Roman Empire Argument* of romantic conservatives. This claims that the Roman Empire declined and fell because it was rotted away by unmentionable vices. The very same vices threaten us today, and therefore by all the rules of analogy our civilization will collapse unless there is a speedy return to "traditional moral standards". The way the argument is used implies a rough equation of immorality with licentiousness, and of morality with self-discipline. Its premisses are dubious, and its logic deplorable: but it has an enduring appeal, especially in periods of Conservative government.

Two utterly different pictures of the past, then: one bigoted and cruel, the other orderly and beautiful. And with these different pictures of the past, contrary evaluations of organized religion: for the freethinker, it is an ugly burden of superstition and intolerance to be thrown off; to the other, it is the guardian of civilization. Each can find evidence in support of his own point of view as readily as rival politicians can interpret events each according to his own ideology.

What is new nowadays is that Christians have themselves increasingly been persuaded by the freethinker's picture of Church history, and are themselves also critical of the form of the Church as they have received it. The main reason for this is that vast changes in Christian ethics have almost destroyed

---

[1] *Leslie Stephen* (1951), and subsequent writings.
[2] See the case made out by "Demopheles" in Schopenhauer's *Dialogue on Religion*: and by Freud's interlocutor in the dialogue in *The Future of an Illusion.*

the moral authority of the Christian past. What may be called the World Council of Churches' package of progressive Christian attitudes on social questions is much closer to the ethic of the French Revolution's National Assembly than to the ethic of the *Ancien Régime*. In his attitudes the modern Christian is closer to William Godwin and Tom Paine, to Bentham and his successors, than to any late-Hanoverian bishop. Modern Christians are inclined to be opposed to racial discrimination, to slavery, to anti-semitism. They are inclined to regard poverty as an evil to be remedied, rather than a holy state of life. They believe in liberal democracy, freedom of expression, female emancipation, social equality. They think contraception to be a positive duty in many cases. They dislike paternalistic or authoritarian forms of government at all levels. But all these ideas have come down to us from the freethinkers, rather than from the Church; so that it is natural that modern Christians should so often have come to share the freethinker's verdict upon the historic institutional Churches. The modern Christian believes that the historic Churches were unable or unwilling to grasp the obvious implications of the Gospel, until the necessary lesson was taught to them by freethinkers or by Quakers.

We must spell this out in a little more detail. *Slavery* would seem to be incompatible with the Gospel. But it is commanded in the Old Testament, accepted in the New, and coexisted with Christianity for eighteen centuries. A predecessor of mine as Dean of Emmanuel, John Cotton, was "converted" and sailed to America where he became one of the earliest slave-owners, as well as founder of a Church and New England's leading theologian.[1] Anglican clergymen kept slaves in the West Indies for nearly two centuries, and a Methodist missionary was hanged in Demerara for preaching abolition as late as 1824. It was not Wilberforce the Christian who pioneered abolition, as popular legend has it. On the contrary, as Wilberforce himself told the Commons on February 18, 1796, revolutionary France had already freed its slaves overseas:

[1] E. S. Shuckburgh, *Emmanuel College* (1904), pp. 45f.; Jean Russell, *God's Lost Cause* (1968), p. 16.

Christian England was not to free them for 37 years. It was the same revolutionary Assembly which gave Jews the citizenship which Christian France had denied them.

Equally instructive is the history of *contraception*. John T. Noonan has told the macabre Catholic story.[1] In modern times it was of course a clergyman, Malthus, who published his *Essay on Population* in 1798 and saw that sooner or later there must be voluntary limitation of populations. He willed the end, but he could propose no more practical means than late marriage and continence. These means may possibly work, but only with the assistance of war, pestilence, famine, and other miseries. It was left to freethinkers to will the means: the open publication of contraceptive knowledge was pioneered by a few brave men, under quaintly euphemistic titles like *The Fruits of Philosophy*. The outstanding display of moral courage among these "neo-Malthusians" was that of Charles Bradlaugh and Annie Besant who in 1877 deliberately provoked, fought, and in the end won, a test case.[2] In all this story not one Christian played any part: the Churches mostly followed generations behind, when it had become inexpedient *not* to change their traditional tune.

What people mean by calling the Churches "reactionary" can be illustrated by the example of *education* in England. By Canon 77 of 1604 no one might teach publicly or privately unless he held the bishop's licence and had made the same form of subscription (to the Articles, etc.) as the clergy make upon ordination. The history of English education thereafter is in large measure the history of the Church's long struggle to save what it could of this position of privilege. Some sided with the Church because they believed in the voluntary principle. In 1807 the Archbishop of Canterbury secured the rejection of Whitbread's Education Bill in the Lords. Shaftesbury was among the opponents of another Bill rejected in 1850. Yet at this time half the population was illiterate, and there was only one grammar school for every 23,000 people, whereas at the Reformation there had been one for every 8,000.

[1] *Contraception : A History of its Treatment by Catholic Theologians and Canonists* (1965).
[2] See the memorial volume, *Charles Bradlaugh : Champion of Liberty* (1933).

Only in 1870, long after France and Germany, was an Education Act passed; and the religious issue has complicated the subsequent Acts of 1902 and 1944, and will still complicate the next.[1]

Time would fail us to tell of other issues, such as the gradual political emancipation of the working class, the gradual social emancipation of women, and the movement of African and Asian peoples towards political independence. But if we were to tell of them, can it be denied that the story would be much the same? Over a very large field of great moral advances the pioneers are much more commonly found to be freethinkers than orthodox Christians. The classical line-up of forces is that which was usual in France: Jews, Protestants and Free-thinkers *versus* the Church, the Army and the upper and middle classes.[2] Churches which place a high value on doctrine, on the clergy and the sacraments, and alliance with the State, are much less likely to be found in the vanguard of social reform than members of a body like the Society of Friends. Take an issue such as the reform of prison conditions, or the reform of the law, and ask yourself which body is more likely to have taken the lead: a pressure group of Quakers and freethinkers, or the bench of bishops? The question answers itself. It is true that in the last 50 years the policy of the bishops on social issues has changed radically: not only in England, but even nowadays in a country like Spain. But that is because they themselves have been influenced by the changes which I am describing.

What has happened, and why is it that since the mid-eighteenth century moral leadership has been in the hands of freethinkers? In a word, the explanation is that the great changes in society in the modern period have all been by-products of secularization. The modern period has been and is broadly egalitarian: one group after another, but particularly the working class, blacks and women, have risen up to claim

[1] For the above paragraph, see W. O. Lester Smith, *Education in Great Britain* (1949).

[2] See, for example, A. Dansette, *Religious History of Modern France* (ET, two vols., 1961).

equal rights. What has made it possible for them to do this has been the overthrow of the old mythical world-picture. The mythical world-picture was always hierarchical, and historic Christianity was integrated with it. The ruling classes were high, noble, the quality: those they ruled were low, base, commoners: male was nobler than female, white was good and black was evil. Man to woman was as sun to moon, white man to black man was as day to night.

The overthrow of the mythical world-picture has been and still is an intensely painful business, leading to a colossal and world-wide social upheaval. Egalitarianism is the most obvious byproduct of it, and radical utilitarianism was its typical intellectual tool. Hence the most secularized groups in society —freethinkers, Quakers, and a few leaders of the unchurched working class—have been best able to see the way and point it out.

Until the end of the nineteenth century the Churches did not fully recognize what was happening. Now they have at least begun the process of dissociating Christianity from the old mythical world-picture. One of the results has been an extraordinary change in Christian social ethics.

Many critics are scornful about this change. It seems to them farcical that the Churches, over a long period and over issues ranging from whether the earth orbits the sun to whether women may be ordained, should so consistently have resisted change till the eleventh hour, and then have abruptly reversed their policy and announced that the opposite of their traditional teaching is after all the obvious corollary of the gospel.

This criticism of the Churches is a mistake. People suppose that Christianity is typically and properly what Augustine, Dante, and Milton, say it is. But even such a passionate lover of the medieval world-picture as the late C. S. Lewis was obliged to point out that it does not always fit very well with Christianity. To the men of the Middle Ages, "their cosmology and their religion were not such easy bed-fellows as might be supposed. At first we may fail to notice this, for the cosmology appears to us, in its firmly theistic basis and its ready welcome to the supernatural, to be eminently religious. And so in one sense it is. But it is not eminently Christian. The Pagan elements

93

embedded in it involved a conception of God, and of man's place in the universe, which, if not in logical contradiction to Christianity, were subtly out of harmony with it."[1] This statement is all the more striking because Lewis might well be thought the last man to make it. I believe it can be claimed that, in slowly dissociating itself from an hierarchical and mythical world-picture, Christianity is laboriously recovering its own integrity, rather than being disingenuous. Thus, in the last two centuries the Churches have been coaxed along by promptings from outside. A socialist critic may say that the Old Testament prophets are closer in spirit to Marxist humanism than to the political theory of St. Thomas Aquinas. Even after the necessary caveats have been entered, such a remark may help the Churches to see their own foundation documents in a new way.

But this process has undoubtedly damaged the Church's pride in its own past.

Church history is written with the benefit of hindsight, and in retrospect the unpopular pioneer whose opinions eventually prevail looks a bigger man than he did to his own contemporaries. So the very way Church history is written may tend to make the historical record appear better than it really was. The historian traces a line of courageous people who were thought insignificant by their contemporaries, but were prophets and pioneers, and in whom the historian therefore perceives the true apostolic succession. There is no calculated dishonesty here. Histories of nineteenth-century thought written before 1914 do not mention Marx or Kierkegaard:[2] histories written today give them a large place. But in Church history the almost inevitable practice of treating certain original figures as being retrospectively of great historical importance is not really compatible with a Catholic doctrine of the Church. Is it not odd that in every age the great weight of the institutional Church, organized religion, should have so unfailingly been exerted on the wrong side? How is this to be reconciled with a high valuation of the institutional side of religion? The practice of writing Church

[1] *The Discarded Image* (1964), pp. 18f.
[2] For example, E. C. Moore, *Christian Thought since Kant* (1912).

history as the record of an irregular line of charismatic individuals, a rather Old Testament practice, began among left-wing Protestants at the Reformation. Nowadays even a Catholic historian might feel compelled to adopt it. It would not be easy nowadays, if one proposed to vindicate the Church by appeal to history, to write Church history as the march through time of a great disciplined army, with the hierarchy in the van.

After all this has been said there remains the question of the oppressiveness and cruelty of organized religion, which troubles many people. It has many aspects. One is the dubious virtue of *zeal*: precisely because it takes itself and its claims so seriously a Church can easily encourage an unreasonable and pitiless fanaticism in its own members, and fail to distinguish between its own self-interest and the claims of what it calls "truth". Ecumenical negotiations constantly illustrate the point: the negotiators are mostly clergymen, the most intractable topic is the doctrine of the ministry, and the negotiations have the air of a struggle between two rival priesthoods, each determined that there shall be no formula of reconciliation which implies any relinquishment of its traditional claims and prerogatives. The language used is the language of power theologically sanctified: *authority, loyalty to tradition, historic ministry, claims of truth*. In Northern Ireland today the popular leaders, Miss Devlin and Mr. Paisley, have in common a total inability to see the other's point of view: a wilfully blind intransigence, which has given zeal a bad name.

Secondly, there is the question of the Church as a kind of *superperson*. In recent years the image of the Church as the Body of Christ has been very popular. But insofar as the members of the Church see themselves as mere cells in the body of a superperson they renounce their own spiritual freedom. They are thus prepared to acquiesce in the ever-popular imagery of shepherd and sheep, the pastor and his flock. But this imagery is morally disastrous. It is unfortunate that in recent years there have been few additions to the literature on religion and the artist's freedom, of which the Gide-Claudel correspondence is an important document. The reason for the gap is probably that nowadays artists freely borrow religious imagery and themes, as they have always done, but it is generally taken for granted that no front-rank artist can live as a loyal member of any Church which imposes a strict discipline on its members. Take, for example, the Irish literary renaissance which began almost a century ago, and which is even yet producing fresh names, such as those of John McGahern, Christy Brown and many others. Every one of these writers is deeply influenced by Catholicism, but every one had in some degree to break away from Catholicism to become a writer.

And so, finally, there is the charge that organized religion is *psychologically oppressive*. Since the Second World War many thinkers popular among students have been attempting to synthesize the legacies of Freud and Marx. They include Sartre, Marcuse and R. D. Laing—not very respectable names, perhaps, but they have helped to catalyse a synthesis of the classic Marxian and Freudian criticisms of organized religion. The synthesis is seldom clearly stated, but it is part of the climate of our time, and I shall attempt to formulate it.

Long ago Plato drew an analogy between the individual and the state, and set a tripartite model of the self alongside a three-class model of society. As reason should govern "spirit" and appetites in the individual, so the wise old men should govern the military and labouring classes in society.

With the Romantic Movement, two revolutions, a psychological and a social, arrived independently. There was an overthrow of the hegemony of reason in the individual soul and a fresh affirmation of the imagination and the passions. Correspondingly, the traditional ruling class was overthrown in society and replaced by the government of the popular will.

But these two rivers flowed along separate channels, for a long time. Even so, parallels remain. People claim that there is a parallel between Marx's dynamic picture of society and Freud's dynamic model of the self. But Freud himself was a social conservative, who did *not* believe that a revolutionary transformation of the self for good might be achieved through the overthrow of the superego by the id.

However, psychoanalysis (especially in America) could

hardly remain content with Freud's own very modest estimate of what it could achieve. In "underground" circles in America and elsewhere there is a widespread belief in the possibility of a kind of double psychological-social revolution. This ideology would not have commended itself to either Freud or Marx themselves: it reminds observers rather of Rousseau or Shelley. But it does spring from a loose synthesis of the two.

The critique of religion which was begun by Hegel, developed by Feuerbach, and completed by Marx, argues that a religious system is nothing but the projected and illusory gratification of hopes and needs which cannot gain satisfaction in the real world.[1] It is rather like a Freudian "substitute gratification" through fantasy, dreaming or artistic expression. The ruling class perceives this, and allegedly purveys religion to the lower classes in order to sublimate political discontent.

Now this analysis has some plausibility when applied to the religions of classical antiquity, and of course Marx had studied Epicurus, a critic of those religions. But it does not explain why the populace so willingly fall into the trap, and why millions remain obstinately Christian in modern Russia.

The suggestion is that Freud's notion of "introjection" supplies the clue. Society uses religion to persuade us to "introject", take into ourselves, the voice of authority, and call it conscience. Society creates an internal conflict within each of us: it implants notions of shame and dread, sin and guilt, and sets us each and all on the path of self-conquest. Religion is its principal instrument, and the invisible inner tyranny it creates is self-perpetuating. For example, suppose I believe in the doctrine of Original Sin: I am inwardly divided, I feel in myself both good and evil impulses, feelings of love and of hate. My child loves me, but, persuaded of the truth of the doctrine of Original Sin, I reckon he is born perverse and unruly, and beat

---

[1] The first statement of this criticism of religion appears in Hegel's *The Spirit of Christianity and its Fate* (1798–99), in *On Christianity: Early Theological Writings*, tr. T. M. Knox and R. Kroner (1948). See pp. 162f. Notice that Hegel here links the cruelties of Christianity with its "objective" conception of God. The pessimism of the decaying Roman Empire was expressed in its sense of man's worthlessness, God's transcendence. Worthless and impotent in himself, the individual's highest destiny was to be another's ruthless instrument.

him. I thus reproduce in him the same conflict between loving feelings and feelings of hate which I experience myself. The doctrine of Original Sin has therefore the great advantage of being both self-verifying and self-propagating. If it can be established in a community it will keep going by its own momentum.

So it is claimed that organized religion seeks to establish a psychological tyranny over men by inculcating anxiety and heightening scruples. It naturally allies itself with repressive forces in society, forces which demand discipline, punishment, censorship, purity, and self-control. In spite of all the old talk about redemption, as a matter of fact, organized religion's social influence is always on the side of containment rather than liberation. A good shepherd keeps control of his flock.

These charges—that the Church has encouraged fanaticism, that it has restricted individual freedom, and that it is psychologically repressive—are very general, and difficult to evaluate. Zeal may be generous and heroic, as well as mean and narrow. As for the alleged stifling oppressiveness of organized religion, we must say this about it: *every* conversion is experienced by the convert as a passage from bondage to freedom, whether it be a conversion *into* religion or a conversion *out of* religion.[1] Susan Budd records that secularist converts from religion came to see the Church as reactionary, corrupt and oppressive: in fact they described the Church they had renounced pretty much as Christian converts describe the world *they* have renounced.

But I propose to admit that there is *some* justice in these charges. The task of evaluating them empirically would surely be impossibly complicated: but we can ask whether the Church's own theology of itself has contained the germs of later corruption. And I shall argue that the root of the trouble has lain in the doctrine of the two cities.

The mainstream of historic Christianity has always stayed true to its apocalyptic origins in being dualistic. Its language creates a series of antitheses, dividing the moral universe into

---

[1] On conversion, see William James, *The Varieties of Religious Experience* (1902); G. W. Allport, *The Individual and his Religion* (1950), etc. On conversion out of Christianity, see Susan Budd's article, cited earlier.

two opposed camps. There is the way of life, the straight and narrow way; and the way of death, which is broad and easy. Every human act is performed under the influence of either God or Satan, and is a step towards Heaven or Hell. There are two societies, the elect whom God loves and has chosen for life, and the reprobate whom God has abandoned to Satan. The Church and the World are two distinct, visibly distinct, societies: and with this distinction, which verges upon a separation, run a series of others, between faith and reason, mercy and justice, Christianity and culture, grace and nature. There is at least a tendency to divide the self into good and evil realms. All that is merely human in us is of the old Adam, of the flesh; all that is of *ourselves* is to be fought: we do well only insofar as we collaborate with grace infused into us from without. The cosmic battle's front lines are within each soul.

Two-cities Christianity takes two forms, according to whether it is a politically impotent minority group in society, or whether it is established as the official religion of the state.

In opposition, so to speak, it takes the form of a sect, a sharply defined sub-group.[1] The sect has its own distinctive vocabulary, and attaches great importance to the procedures by which people are admitted to or expelled from membership. Since it makes a sharp distinction between those inside and those outside its membership, the sect makes no pretence of being a great reconciling force in society. On the contrary, its existence often presents the state with serious problems. A stateman's task is to discover, appeal to, and build upon some kind of moral consensus among all the citizens. The state is trying to unite the citizenry, but the sect's theology asserts a division among them. If then the state, pursuing its proper objectives, seeks to contain and limit the divisive effects of the sect's activities, the sect complains that it is suffering persecution. In some measure the sect must be in opposition to the state, and so is encouraged to identify itself with the cause of other oppressed groups. Though the sect is clearly in some ways socially harmful, it does at least remain true to its own origins among the oppressed, and through its eschatological doctrines

[1] A protestant sect like the Jehovah's Witnesses is a good contemporary example.

it gives hope to many people whose worldly situation is almost hopeless.

If the sect be suddenly elevated to a position of political power, and given opportunity to make itself co-extensive with the state, very substantial changes in the way it applies its doctrines are called for. They are made with disconcerting readiness.[1] The sect's hostility had formerly been directed against those outside its membership, and above all against the state itself. The Church preached a "transvaluation of values". It rejected the public value-system and the social hierarchy which embodied it, declaring that the mighty would be thrust from their seats, and the humble and base exalted to replace them. The Church's value-system was precisely the reverse of the world's, and it announced the imminent over-throw of the state, declaring that the last would be first and the first last. But when the Church comes to power it finds itself allied with its former enemies: the mighty, the rich, the military. Hostility must be redirected. In alliance with the state-power the Church must now turn its hostility against those who dissent from or reject the new Christian order.

So when it is in power two-cities Christianity sanctifies the penal system, the armed forces and all those who bear authority. It now sees the apparatus of human vengeance, human "justice", not as working in opposition to divine judge-ment but as instruments of it. The religion of a condemned criminal, rejected of men, now itself condemns criminals in his name.

No one has felt the irony of this change more deeply than Leo Tolstoy, whose novel *Resurrection* expresses his sense of outrage at the Russian penal system in the last years of the Tsarist régime. It is not surprising that a full text of this novel was not published for 30 years: the censor had reasons for being dissatisfied. The ruling class are portrayed as indolent and selfish, and being without religion are given up to the grossest superstition, like the General who leaves his table-turning impatiently in order to refuse a simple humanitarian request,[2]

[1] The classic document is Eusebius of Caesarea's *Life of Constantine*.
[2] Part II, 19.

or the ladies who are affected by a sentimental *salon* evangelist.[1] The Church's worship is corrupt,[2] and it leaves the soul of a conforming believer deeply dissatisfied.[3] The ruling Procurator of the Holy Synod, Pobedonostsev, appears in the novel thinly disguised as a monster of cruel cynicism.[4] Those who think this portrait grotesque need only refer to a biography of Tolstoy to learn something of the character of the historical Procurator.[5] But most horrible of all is the association of Christ with the cruel legal system by which the ruling class maintains its power. This class may be idle and cruel, but it still has enough cunning to use the image of the Crucified in defence of its own interests. The clergy bless the proceedings of the courts; they hang crucifixes in rooms where terrible injustices are done, as if in calculated mockery; and the celebration of the Orthodox Liturgy in the prison helps to persuade decent men that God intends and approves their becoming heartless officials, and their victims that their sufferings are somehow deserved and expiatory.[6]

This has been, historically, the most deeply-felt objection to "organized religion": that when two-cities Christianity is in power it so readily becomes tyrannical, and in everything it does seems untrue to its own origins among the oppressed. Tolstoy's successor, Alexander Solzhenitsyn, has made a very similar criticism of the Stalinist corruption of Marxism, in his novel, *The First Circle*: and it has even become a popular *mot* that all great institutions end by subverting the ideals in whose name they were founded.

So, two-cities Christianity can appear unattractive, whether in government or in opposition. In government, it contradicts

---

[1] Part II, 17.
[2] Part I, 38f.
[3] Part II, 23.
[4] Part II, 27.
[5] E. J. Simmons, *Leo Tolstoy* (1949).
[6] Part I, 39. See a further collection of Tolstoy's writings on the Church in *Essays and Letters*, tr. Aylmer Maude (World's Classics, 1903, etc.). On the presence of the clergy at executions, see Albert Camus, "Reflections on the Guillotine", in *Resistance Rebellion and Death* (1961): "those who have placed at the very centre of their faith the overwhelming victim of a judicial error should appear more reticent, to say the least, when confronted by cases of judicial murder."

its own teaching by its behaviour: in opposition, it is anti-social, for the drive of its theology tends to undermine the moral consensus of all citizens which statesmen must try to develop. Two-cities Christianity is basically a divisive, not a reconciling, presence in society, especially when it goes so far as to refuse to acknowledge political obligation, repudiate natural reason and morality, and teach limited atonement. It brings, not peace, but a sword.

Most commentators prefer two-cities Christianity in opposition because it is in that situation at least true to its origins and internally morally coherent.[1] But, either way, there are real moral objections to it.

So there have always been some one-city theologians. They look back, perhaps, to Clement and Origen, to some of the Antiochene theologians, and (if they are brave) to those good men, the later Pelagians. The one-city theologians are sometimes described as liberals or humanists, and they have stood for some kind of continuity between faith and reason, Christianity and culture, church and creation, grace and nature. Their succession is a miscellaneous line of men: Abélard, Erasmus, Zwingli, Socinus, Castellio, Chillingworth, the Cambridge Platonists, Locke. Among all these men you will find hardly anyone whom the Church has reckoned a saint, and many whom it has called outright heretics. It is fair to comment that extreme dualists, like Tertullian and Kierkegaard, have not been canonized either: but it is nevertheless true to say that what the community has in all ages regarded as orthodox has been two-cities Christianity rather than one-city Christianity. Church history has been written in such a way as to suggest that a two-city man like Luther is a greater figure than his one-city opponent Erasmus. The intransigent seems the more typically and centrally Christian figure, and Kierkegaard is deemed more edifying to read than F. R. Tennant.

And the reason for this is the demand of the Church for an ideology which will explain and justify its own distinct existence. One-city men have often flourished in academic circles, but it is

[1] E.g. Walter Kaufmann, in *The Faith of a Heretic* (1961), Chapter IX: "Organized Religion".

the two-city men who are closer to the heart of the Church. The formation of a theology is something like the formation of a political programme, and one-city theologies are like otherwise admirable political ideologies which lack that one thing necessary, a strong class or interest basis. One-city Christianity is always accused of lacking "cutting edge", of being vague or woolly: it lacks the power to create an enduring distinct community.

Being what it is, the Church demands of a theologian that he produce a theology which will consolidate its own membership by telling them that they know things which outsiders do not know, that they have a unique mission, that they have a destiny from which outsiders are excluded, that they have, as a body, a *raison d'être*. For the sake of its own morale, for the sake of its very survival as a distinct body, the Church demands a two-cities theology. When people lose faith in Hell they begin to wonder what the Church is for, and why it is urgent that the Gospel be preached. These are facts, and it is idle to pretend otherwise. Theologians, says the Church, exist to serve the Church, and what they say is "true" if it makes the Church strong. To make the Church strong you must prove that it matters a great deal whether people belong to the Church or not and you must show that through the labours of the Church people can be rescued from damnation. The Church says that a great theologian is a man who revitalizes the Church: so it promises an immortal memory to the man who makes a compelling two-cities theology. The one-city man who grows on the academical margin of the Church can never play a central part in its life, because the very nature of the visible body of Christ is such that it demands a separate identity and a two-cities theology.

The original imagery in which the Church was described adequately suggests what has proved to be its enduring character. It was an ark in which a few were rescued from the general destruction; a bundle of pieces of wood snatched from the general conflagration; a chosen people composed of an elect few, picked out from every nation. It was never entirely happy to sink itself in the life of a whole society, like Hinduism or Islam.

It has always had a need to assert its own distinctness, its independence of the fortunes of nations: it saw itself as the only continuing city, the one and only society against which the gates of hell would not prevail. It contemplated the collapse of empires with equanimity, and even with satisfaction, for the great disasters of history served only to verify its own fundamental doctrine of the two cities.

So, I have charged the Church with exercising a deforming influence upon the history of theology. As soon as it becomes conscious of itself as a distinct body it demands a two-cities ideology to justify its distinctness. But a two-cities theology strengthens the Church community only at the price of dividing mankind into two opposed camps. Love of the brethren, *philadelphia*, is purchased at the price of detestation of those without, *xenophobia*. The resulting emotion is very like what, in a secularized form, came to be known as *nationalism*. The analogy is close: as the nation-state hates traitors even more than it hates enemies, so the Church hates apostates and heretics even more than it hates infidels. And the Church may strengthen itself by stirring up popular hostility against Islam, against the Jew, the heretic, or the witch, rather as a weak nation-state points out scapegoats or issues a call to arms to divert internal unrest.

But one-city Christianity is politically weak, because, like political liberalism, it is short on enemies. A one-city theology like that of F. D. Maurice demythologizes away the wrath of God. It makes the Church coextensive with creation. It says that all mankind belong to Christ, all are redeemed by him, and all things will be consummated in him. Such a theology has made a good deal of headway in modern times, and not only in Anglicanism: and it has inevitably led to a certain diffuseness, and to doubts about the *raison d'être* of the Church and its stipendiary clergy.

The equation, once again, is difficult to balance. But my own conclusion is that two-cities Christianity, with its strong ecclesiology and dualistic outlook, has had morally bad effects. A one-city Christianity, with a weak ecclesiology, is very much to be preferred. Indeed, in the century in which electronic communications have begun to create citizens of the world, and the hope of a united mankind, it is now the only serious possibility. The old two-cities Christianity is fast becoming a disagreeable anachronism.

6

IMAGERY OF DOMINATION
AND SUBMISSION

THE LANGUAGE of the great monotheistic religions—Judaism, Christianity and Islam—is shot through with imagery of domination and submission. God is described as King, Lord, Judge, and Father, and the believer appears before him as subject, servant, defendant and obedient child. A popular (though perhaps mistaken) etymology has it that *religio* is the *ligamentum*, the system of bonds by which the servant is bound in obedience to his divine master. And these bonds are tight. As God is King of kings and Lord of lords he surpasses the believer infinitely, making a demand infinitely more compelling than the demand of any earthly authority. God is the sole absolute Lord and proprietor of everything. In him is all power and perfection, in us is all weakness and baseness. Before him we can never be in the right: we can only abase ourselves in adoration.

In the past, it might be thought, such language did not create any particular problem. The classic example is Aristotle's treatment of slavery in the *Politics*. To Aristotle, the universe in every part exhibits the relation of ruler and ruled: every composite whole is hierarchically ordered and that which is naturally superior rules that which is naturally inferior.[1] Form rules matter, soul rules body, male rules female, intellect rules appetite, and master rules slave. And in each case the rule is in the best interests of both parties. Among men it is, Aristotle thinks, a matter of fact that some are born to rule and some are born to be ruled. Domination and submission is the law of the universe.

[1] Book I.

However, even in Aristotle's account there are certain reservations. First, many actual slaves are people captured in war. If Greeks think it just to have barbarian slaves why should not barbarians think it just to enslave captured Greeks? But no Greek thinks that a Greek ought to be a slave. Aristotle acknowledges that some philosophers think that slavery is unjust. Again, slaves are, after all, men and not tools. Insofar as a slave can understand his master's intentions, follow an argument, and so forth, he is rational. But if a slave is rational he is surely capable of framing and executing *his own* intentions? How is this compatible with being a natural slave? And, in the third place, Aristotle desires that the relations of masters and slaves be humanely ordered, and as part of this says[1] that slaves ought always to have a hope of emancipation.[1] But this is not compatible with the notion of a "natural slave".

So there are serious objections to Aristotle's account of slavery, objections which he himself saw. Nevertheless, he continued to insist that some men are naturally superior to others, and have a right to rule them, and there is no doubt that the rule of superiors over inferiors runs right through his philosophy.

In his famous book, *The Great Chain of Being*,[2] A. O. Lovejoy described some aspects of the old hierarchical world-picture, and described one of the characteristics of the Chain as "linear gradation". This was something of an oversimplification. In fact there were many different hierarchies, at least in the social realm, and they could cut across each other. Though inferior in one, you might be superior in another. The old hierarchically-ordered societies had certain beauties which are (for obvious reasons) underestimated today, and they were not so rigid as we might think. And if someone says baldly that theism makes men servile, the generalization is obviously false. Since God is a Lord infinitely superior to any human lord his claims relativize distinctions between men. It has been very common since Marx for people to say that God is used to sanctify the social hierarchy: his is the supreme Lordship which validates all lesser lordships. The truth was in fact more complicated. Since every human

[1] Book VII (1330ª32).
[2] 1936.

being was able to say "We ought to obey God rather than men", any one could invoke God's claims *against* the claims of any earthly authority. It is historically false to represent religion as having always used the authority of God to endorse human authority. On the contrary, every great monotheistic tradition is a record of men who in the name of God stood up against human authority.

Again, as a matter of experience, God does not appear to enforce his absolute Lordship in any simple and direct way. Perhaps in the past people have thought of him as doing so. Like the Deuteronomic historians in Israel, they reckoned that if you failed to obey God your fortunes would quickly and visibly decline; and if you served him diligently you could be sure of prosperity. But close observers even then doubted whether experience bore out this generalization.[1] God's absolute Lordship is rather something posited by human faith than something observed by human eyes.

Furthermore, the language of Lordship can be used in religion by people who cannot be convicted of any desire to validate human dominion over other human beings. For example, hippies today, who are anarchists, have no hesitation in calling Krishna Lord.

So if speaking of God as Lord and Master of men raises doubts in our minds today, we must avoid oversimplification.

The classic statement of a moral objection to monotheism as servile is that of Hegel, and in order to apprehend what the difficulty really is we shall have to examine his opinions, and how it was that he came to hold them. I suggest that Hegel inherited from his predecessors three main lines of thought which led him to his fundamental criticism of monotheism. They were: (a) "the positivity of Christianity"; (b) dislike of an "objective" conception of God; and (c) reaction against a rule-obedience model of morality. In the first of these Hegel adopted Kant's opinion; in the second he transformed Kant's opinion; and in the third he rejected Kant's teaching. In the young Hegel's thought these three lines of criticism coalesced and led him to his denial of the adequacy of monotheism.

[1] As witness, Job's replies to his comforters.

One of Hegel's early manuscripts is an essay on "The Positivity of the Christian Religion", written in various stages between 1795 and 1800.[1] He sets himself what seems at first an odd problem—how did Christianity become the positive religion of a Church?[2] The way he poses his problem presumes that Jesus himself did not preach a positive religion, and that Christianity's becoming a positive religion was a disaster. As for a definition of the term "positive religion", Hegel offers this: "a religion which is grounded in authority, and puts man's worth not at all, or at least not wholly, in morals".[3] Jesus himself had denounced the "moral superstition", typical of positive religions, that the demands of the moral law could be satisfied by observance of the ordinances of religion. Indeed, for the young Hegel, what is commanded authoritatively *cannot* be moral. Jesus "urged not a virtue grounded on authority (which is either meaningless or a direct contradiction in terms), but a free virtue springing from man's own being".[4]

This antithesis between the positive and the moral, Hegel had learnt from Kant's book, *Religion within the Limits of Reason Alone*,[5] published in the same year (1793) that the cult of Reason was set up in Paris. Kant himself used the word "statutory" rather than "positive". For Kant, there can only be one true religion, which is purely rational and moral, and binds all men everywhere equally. An historical faith, with merely statutory laws, can only bind so far as it has been disseminated by human agency. It cannot possibly be the one true universal religion.[6] All God wills for men is that they shall do their duty: but the statutory ecclesiastical faiths add extra non-moral duties, under the influence of a crude anthropomorphism. They suppose that God has ordained a special cult of divine worship: that God commands men to serve him, not merely by doing their duty,

---

[1] *On Christianity: Early Theological Writings by Friedrich Hegel*, trr. T. M. Knox and R. Kroner (1948, Torchbook edn. 1961). This book is cited hereafter as "Hegel" and a page number.

[2] Hegel, pp. 67, 71ff.

[3] *ibid.*, p. 71.

[4] *ibid.*

[5] Tr. by T. M. Greene and H. H. Hudson (1934, Harper Torchbook edn. 1960). This book is cited hereafter as "Kant" and a page number.

[6] Kant, pp. 94ff., etc.

but also by special observances of a non-moral, purely positive kind. And this Kant thinks evil.[1]

Hegel perhaps learnt to use the word "positive" from Lessing, who uses it in the Introduction to his tract *The Education of the Human Race* (1780). But behind Lessing and Kant stand the English Deists. The simplest early statement of the case against positive religion is that of Charles Blount.[2] He sets out the argument in a syllogism:

> That Rule which is necessary to our future Happiness, ought to be generally made known to all men.
>
> But no Rule of Revealed Religion was, or ever could be, made known to all men.
>
> Therefore no Revealed Religion is necessary to future Happiness.
>
> The Major is thus prov'd:
>
> Our Future Happiness depends upon our obeying, or endeavouring to fulfil the known Will of God.
>
> But that Rule which is not generally known cannot be generally obey'd.
>
> Therefore that Rule which is not generally known, cannot be the Rule of our Happiness.
>
> Now the Minor of the first Syllogism is a matter of Fact . . . no Religion supernatural has been conveyed to all the World. . . .

And Blount goes on to answer the theory that God will judge Christians by the Gospel and infidels by the precepts of Natural Religion. He says that Natural Religion is either sufficient for salvation or it is not: if it is, then Revelation is superfluous; but, if it is not, then God is unjust in that some people by geographical chance are denied knowledge essential to their eternal happiness.

Behind Blount again stands the medieval distinction between natural and positive law, but the difficulty is by now clear. The suggestion is that insofar as a religion is positive it is not purely moral. What is moral is universal, what is positive has a historical origin and is peculiar to a certain community. The existing positive religions obviously contain truly moral elements

[1] Kant, p. 142n., etc.
[2] *The Oracles of Reason* (1693), no. 14. Reprinted in J. M. Creed and J. S. Boys Smith, *Religious Thought in the Eighteenth Century* (1934), pp. 23f.

but they are always tempted to stress their peculiar laws, the kind of observance which the modern critic might (inaccurately) call a "taboo". And this leads to all kinds of evil. Kant could hardly have put his case more strongly: virtue, pursued for its own sake, leads to godliness; but godliness pursued for its own sake, leads not to virtue but rather to "a fawning slavish subjection to a despotically commanding might".[1] The idea that God requires anything else but moral obedience he calls "fetichism", "religious illusion", "pseudo-service", "devotional hypocrisy", and he thinks the clergy have a particular interest in encouraging such illusions.

Kant's hatred of "positivity" was so great that he does not pause long enough to explain how it arose. Hegel suggests that among the Jews it was a product of their desire for isolation, and their detestation of neighbouring peoples. In the face of foreign influences they "clung all the more obstinately to the statutory commands of their religion; they derived their legislation directly from a jealous God . . . Of spirit nothing remained save obstinate pride in slavish obedience."[2]

Hegel's remarks betray something of eighteenth-century anti-Jewish cliché: it is interesting to reflect that a good deal of anti-monotheistic polemic derives from anti-Jewish writing, just as many anti-Christian arguments derive historically from anti-Catholic polemics. But Hegel has a point. Monotheism is surely a universal faith: but the religions of Jew, Sikh and Muslim are sharply divided. Why is this? Surely because of an irrational concentration on divisive positive ordinances—the five pillars of Islam, the five books of Moses. The combination of monotheism with xenophobia is always odd. "In the jealous God of Abraham and his posterity there lay the horrible claim that He alone was God and that this nation was the only one to have a god."[3]

The second strand in Hegel's criticism of monotheism is the dislike of "an objective conception of God". Here he began from Kant, and went beyond him. There are two places in Kant's

[1] Kant, pp. 171f.
[2] Hegel, p. 177f.
[3] Hegel, p. 188.

Religion where he suggests that if religion is to remain pure God must not, as it were, become too real. In the first, Kant says that, in a perfectly proper sense we all do and must *"create a God for ourselves"* according to moral concepts. Even if an alleged revelation be set before us, we must first compare it with this ideal. "There can be no religion springing from revelation alone, that is without *first* positing that concept, in its purity, as a touchstone. Without this all reverence for God would be *idolatry*."[1]

Secondly, in discussing prayer, Kant says that prayer to an objective God is superstition. In this kind of prayer God is imagined literally present, and the believer takes up an appropriate posture, perhaps even speaking aloud. His prayer is a stated wish; he is even trying to bend God's will. But this is superstition. True prayer, the only prayer which can be made in faith, and is sure to be heard, consists simply in a heartfelt desire to do our duties as if in God's service. We invoke the *idea* of God in framing our resolve. And this prayer can be made quite sincerely by someone who is not certain of God's existence.[2]

Kant's criticism of an objective deity was that a God so thought of might be approached in non-moral ways. Hegel's objection, first apparent in *The Spirit of Christianity* (and in an earlier fragment on *Love*) is that an objective God must be alien.

Hegel supposed that the divine had originally been immanent within men. Like the Romantics, he idealized the Greeks and denigrated the Jews. Antiquity eventually fell into monotheism out of despair. The despotism of the Roman Emperors created a climate in which men despaired of earthly happiness. The divine in man took flight, and found refuge in another world. Theism in all forms makes a fundamental distinction between man and God, and as such is a manifestation of man's alienation from his own infinite spiritual nature. It has been urged, by M. B. Foster[3] and others, that theism helped to make technology

---

[1] Kant, p. 157n. See also p. 101n., on expounding the Bible according to morality, and not *vice versa*.

[2] Kant, p. 183n. See also p. 142n., where "It is possible that there may be a God" is declared to be subjectively sufficient: any stronger conviction is morally risky, for it could lead to "pseudo-service", or "courtly" rituals.

[3] "The Christian Doctrine of Creation and the Rise of Modern Natural Science", *Mind*, Vol. XLIII, N.S., pp. 446f. (1934).

possible. Hegel anticipated this argument very interestingly. The Jewish patriarchs struggled to control their environment, objectifying the not-self and trying to bring it under the control of thought. They did this by imagining a God who held the world completely in his sway. Submitting to that ideal, the servants of God hoped to master the world. But the price was alienation from both the world and God, manifested in the loss of appreciation of natural beauty, and a God whose restless power never allowed his worshippers any real participation in his divinity.[1] Hegel's romantic belief that technology is associated with alienation from the world and God survived into the twentieth century in writers like Heidegger.

Hegel's nature treatment of the sorrows of monotheism is contained in Chapter 4 of *The Phenomenology of Spirit*.[2] He begins with his celebrated analysis of the Master–slave relationship. In contrast with Aristotle he treats the relation dynamically, and in a way which strongly suggests that the master is the worse off of the two. Each, in a way, lives vicariously through the other: but it is the slave who sees himself reflected in one higher than himself. And the master degenerates into a mere parasite. The slave is in a more immediate and productive contact with the physical world: in time he must come to realize his own greater strength, see that his master is redundant, and overthrow him.

In the same chapter occurs Hegel's famous description of the "Unhappy Consciousness" of medieval Christianity: unhappy because it consists in a dualism of two worlds, earth and heaven. It is discontented with this world, and ceaselessly aspires after the next, which it cannot attain. Its most extreme and morbid manifestation is asceticism. Hegel has hardly more sympathy with the monks than Gibbon and Hume: like them he sees in the monastic life grovelling subjection to a tyrannical deity.

Hegel in fact criticizes theism from the point of view of Pantheism. He wishes to see the depersonalizing of God and the

[1] Hegel, pp. 182ff.
[2] 1807 (tr. J. B. Baillie as *The Phenomenology of Mind*, 1934). On Hegel, see J. N. Findlay's *Hegel* (1958); Walter Kaufmann's *Hegel* (1966); and "The Young Hegel and Religion", in *From Shakespeare to Existentialism* (1959, revised edition 1960).

subsumption of all finite persons and processes into the infinite polycentric divine life. Once allow God a distinct personal centre of his own, and he will rise and expel us from heaven. In fact Hegel thought that the decisive revolutions had already taken place in his own time: the slaves were rising to overthrow their masters. The phrase "God is dead" occurs more than once in his writings: the dead God is the alien, slavemaster God, who must be overcome so that men can re-enter heaven.

The final strand in Hegel's break with monotheism is his rejection of the rule-obedience model of morality. I am constantly surprised at the extent to which, at the present time, people think of morality as a matter of obeying rules, and nothing else. Hegel, following Kant, and living under the shadow of Protestantism, reacted against rule-obedience moralities. At first he drew upon the idealized Greeks for his alternative, seeking in them a morality which was not a matter of obeying but a way of being. But later, in the *Phenomenology*, he described all forms of moralistic consciousness as being transcended in the Religious Consciousness: and he describes this latter state—one of mutual forbearance and acceptance—in terms whose inspiration is plainly Christian. Certainly, for Hegel, moralism is alienation: not only between the human moral agent, the moral law, and the legislator, but also between the natural realm and the moral. The world process is a continuum: ethical monotheism cuts it up into blacks and whites.

Hegel's attempt to "overcome" the European tradition of monotheism is complex, then, and his successors have developed various aspects of it.

Ludwig Feuerbach[1] elaborated Hegel's theory of projection. God is man's own infinite spiritual nature, and the transcendence of God is simply man's alienation from himself. The birth of Christianity, Christian mysticism, and the Reformation, are stages on the way to Humanism, man's reconciliation with his own divine self.

Feuerbach failed to take up Hegel's explanation of how the original alienation had come about. The crucial passage in

[1] *The Essence of Christianity* (1841; ET, George Eliot, 1854); *Lectures on the Essence of Religion* (1851; ET, Ralph Mannheim, 1967).

The Spirit of Christianity[1] was not published till 1907.[2] Marx had a better knowledge of the religions of antiquity, and their political function. In his *Theses on Feuerbach* (1845; published in a slightly different version by Engels, 1888) Marx argues that the religious self-alienation of men must be traced back to "contradictions" (by which he presumably means ills and injustices) in secular society. Only when these "contradictions" are understood and removed in practice will religious self-alienation disappear.[3]

The notion that religious ethics is a "slave-morality" was greatly elaborated by Nietzsche in numerous books.[4] His critique resembled Hegel's in its idealization of the Greeks: and he gave a kind of psychological explanation of how a slave-morality was foisted upon the ancient world by the guile of early Christian apologists.

Kierkegaard, who was much more of a Hegelian than he himself admitted, accepts to a remarkable extent Hegel's charge that the believer in a transcendent God must be unhappy. Indeed he outdoes Luther in the vehemence of his language. The "infinite qualitative difference" between God and man means that love between two such disparate lovers must be a cause of suffering. "To be a Christian is the most terrible of all torments . . . One shudders to read what an animal must suffer which is used for vivisection; yet this is only a fugitive image of the suffering involved in being a Christian. . . ." "If I am . . . flesh and blood . . . then spirit is the most terrible thing for me, terrible as death, and to love spirit is the most terrible thing of all."[5] But we must reserve for separate discussion the question whether Christianity on the whole makes people unhappy, or worse off in this world, and if so how far that is a moral objection to it.

Freud always thought there was something unmanly in religion: he thought that the ego should struggle unflinchingly and

---

[1] Hegel, pp. 162f.

[2] H. Nohl, *Hegels Theologische Jugendschriften*.

[3] *Theses on Feuerbach*, IV: in *Selected Writings in Sociology and Social Philosophy*, edd. T. B. Bottomore and M. Rubel (1956; Pelican edn., 1963).

[4] Such as *The Genealogy of Morals* (1887).

[5] *Journals* XI² A 422, 426; in *The Last Years*, tr. R. Gregor Smith (1965).

without the support of illusions against the harsh demands of external reality. Religious faith was obsessional,[1] feminine,[2] or childish,[3] the product of a neurotic craving for authority. Freud cared not a fig for philosophical theology: as a psychologist, he was interested in the old gross anthropomorphisms that move our emotions. God, for him, was male, a parent, protective but jealous, fierce and demanding. Mysticism was infantile mother-fixation, and Freud never romanticized infancy.

Freud subordinated religion to culture. He thought instinct was at war with culture: culture had progressed, in the past at least, by using religion to sublimate or repress potentially destructive instinctual drives. "In the development of the ancient religions one seems to find that many things which mankind had renounced as wicked were surrendered in favour of the god, and were still permitted in his name; so that a yielding up of evil and asocial impulses to the divinity was the means by which man freed himself from them. For this reason it is surely no accident that all human characteristics—along with the crimes they prompt—were freely attributed to the ancient gods, and no anomaly that it was nevertheless not permissible to justify ones own misdeeds by reference to divine example."[4] There is thus a complete moral disjunction between God and man: "Vengeance is mine, I will repay, saith the Lord." Freud is obviously poles apart from Hegel: but at least he agrees in seeing monotheism as alienation. God is, for Freud, very strongly *over against* Man: subjection to him is frustration, from which rituals give some slight relief. For Freud, as for Hegel, a theistic believer lacks self-knowledge, in the proper German sense of that word. In English "self-consciousness" carries overtones of shame and anxiety: but the German *selbstbewusst sein* is more like the English "self-possession": it means being self-assured and self-confident.[5] For both Hegel and Freud, the old imagery of God as Lord,

---

[1] "Obsessive Acts and Religious Practices" (1907), reprinted in *Collected Papers* II (1924), pp. 25–35.

[2] Philip Rieff, *Freud: The Mind of the Moralist* (1960; Methuen Paperback, 1965), pp. 267f. This is the best short account of Freud's views on religion.

[3] *The Future of an Illusion* (E.T. 1928), pp. 41f.

[4] From the paper on "Obsessive Acts", cited above.

[5] Walter Kaufmann, *Hegel* (1966), p. 152.

Father, Master, King, or Judge, if taken to heart, is incompatible with a human being's proper sense of himself.

Lest we suppose that these criticisms belong only to a certain context, that of German culture since Hegel, we might end this review by citing an author from a totally different tradition:

> It seems likely that this immorality of all the gods so far invented is not an accident, but a necessary consequence of the religious impulse. It is probably connected with the element of worship in religion. One cannot abase oneself before a perfectly moral person, because a perfectly moral person treats one as an equal and as having a right to one's way of life.[1]

But now we must draw a line and begin to evaluate the large body of criticism of monotheism which we have sketched. It is first necessary summarily to dispose of a great deal of sorry nonsense to which we have patiently given a hearing. It will not do to use "the Greeks" as a blank canvas on which any idle dream can be painted; and it will not do to denigrate the Jews. Generation after generation of able men simply passed unthinkingly from hand to hand clichés about the Jews being "sullen", "obstinate", "proud", and hating the human race, and their God being "cruel", "tyrannical", and the like. Only a generation ago people were saying that there could not be a state of Israel because Jews are not good at fighting! The old heroes of faith were not servile characters: men like Elijah and Luther, whatever their other faults, were not obsequious before earthly authority. Natural religion, supposed by eighteenth-century writers to be purely rational, moral, universal, and superior to Christianity, never existed. Those who tried to establish it in modern times merely created fresh sects.

To Hegel it must be replied that not every distinction between two things is an antagonism between them. The overworked word "alienation" smudges the distinction between distinction and antagonism. Mystical communion with God has existed even in those forms of monotheism which most sharply distinguish God and man, such as Islam. The Middle Ages were not so gloomy as Hegel pretended, as is shown by the fact that their

[1] Richard Robinson, *An Atheist's Values* (1964), p. 138.

characteristic artistic form was not a human tragedy but the divine comedy. The monks need no defending: no one who has read the Cistercians could suppose them all to be sick-minded masochists. Technology does not mean alienation from the world, nor need monotheism empty the natural order of divinity. Urban men were the first lovers of natural beauty and to this day are still its most zealous votaries. Christian morality has always been a way of being, an ecstasy of thanksgiving and love. St. Francis' *Canticle of the Sun* is a better expression of it than the sour emphasis on guilt and rules which has sometimes characterized Christianity in its phases of decline. Marx's theory of religion is wrong. Religion joyfully informs the life of many primitive societies to which none of his "contradictions" can plausibly be ascribed. Kierkegaard's last utterances, though wonderfully eloquent, are more those of a Romantic poet in love with suffering than those of a Christian. In his most nearly Christian writings he sings a different tune.[1] Freud's views on religion are largely sheer prejudice, though they make sense in relation to (say) some modern Irish Catholicism, or some kinds of late Victorian Protestantism. But it is perfectly compatible with Christian theology that a good deal of empirical Christianity should be corrupt. Freud should have recalled a famous tale from Boccaccio.[2]

So, much to which we have given a hearing is absurd, though it has been highly influential. What remains is largely a problem of the stifling character of some at least of monotheism's anthropomorphic imagery.

Two points of fact I propose to grant without further dispute. The first is that the basic imagery of God as Father, Judge, King, Lord, and so on, has changed remarkably little over three millenia. It has changed little even though these social functions have varied a great deal. Kings, for example, are not what they were. Even though we may wish to argue against Freud that a religion is more than its anthropomorphic imagery, we must certainly grant to him that the old images are extra-ordinarily tenacious. Attempts to modify them, such as the

[1] Especially the beautiful *Christian Discourses* (1848; ET, 1940).
[2] *Decameron*, Day 1, Novel II.

various American attempts to democratize God, seem bathetic.[1] That they *have* failed does not, however, show that they *must* fail.

The second point I grant is that much in this imagery, rooted as it is in social conditions now long vanished, causes acute discomfort or embarrassment. We feel this embarrassment when presented with a modern translation of the Bible, or modern prayers. The modern idiom is well-meaningly introduced in the hope of bringing Christian faith to life, reviving its emotional impact. The attempt backfires, because it makes the archaisms more obvious, and we are repelled. The drive of historic orthodoxy is always against any sort of "synergism", the doctrine that the natural human will can fruitfully work alongside the divine. All power and goodness is in or from God; all weakness and baseness in men. Men are utterly dependent upon Grace: the language always seems to be turning men into sheep, not sheep into men, even at the price of moral absurdity. If one reads straight through the Collects proper to the seasons in a Roman, Lutheran, or English, service-book (they are substantially the same, and are ancient), one receives an overwhelming impression of man as frail, sinful, morally-impotent, and needing at all times constant benevolent superintendence and protection. The strictly ethical difficulties to which the language of orthodoxy gives rise have been extensively discussed.[2] In essence, the more seriously the imagery of lordship and servanthood be taken the more it diminishes the believer's moral stature. If the believer, in his enthusiasm, declares that of himself he is depraved, that he cannot tell right from wrong, that he can do no good thing, that God must enlighten his conscience, fortify his will, direct his path, inspire and assist all his acts—then such language, the more literally it be taken, the more it offends against our post-Kantian sense of ourselves as responsible moral

[1] C. H. Dodd, *The Interpretation of the Fourth Gospel* (1953), p. 4n. quotes an American labour leader expounding John 5:17: "My father is a working man to this day, and I am one myself." The text *can* be so translated! More serious democratizing of God goes on in such writers as E. S. Brightman and the Process theologians.

[2] For example, W. G. MacLagan, *The Theological Frontiers of Ethics* (1961); P. H. Nowell-Smith, "Morality Religious and Secular", in *Christian Ethics and Contemporary Philosophy*, ed. I. T. Ramsey (1966).

agents. But much of historic orthodoxy, especially where the doctrines of sin and grace are concerned, *has* taken such language very literally.

So the difficulty over Master–servant imagery remains. In the world we have lost, if I were an ordinary man, I would have a larger life and would be better off in the service of some great man than by being my own master. In the world we have lost, the relation between vassal and lord, common soldier and general, was laden with a depth of meaning which we now recall with difficulty. Nowadays a man feels he ought, so far as possible, to be his own master. Nowadays secular acts of homage, prayer and obeisance have largely disappeared: we do not much care to address our fellow men in such ways any more. But that has left the religious forms of these acts rather isolated. What is more, to cling to the old imagery as being the best available strongly suggests that religious people regard the social order which that imagery reflects as the best form of society, because it was the form of society which best imaged the nature of God.

As a way of influencing our superiors, a petition seems nowadays rather genteel and ineffectual. Direct action is better. It is better to trust one's own determination and resourcefulness, than to try to move preoccupied rulers to act by words alone. It is better to irrigate and fertilize the fields than to pray for a good harvest. The way we think about politics and the way we think about prayer are related. Master–servant imagery suggests that we still live in a universe in which petition is the ordinary fellow's best recourse. And this is not true, either in the political or in the natural realms.

What the believer wants to express is his sense of the all-encompassing total adequacy and beauty of God, and the overriding character of God's claims, promises and consolations. He wants to convey a sense of fullness and completeness, experienced in an ecstasy that frees him from himself. It was, formerly, right to express this by saying that he found himself in the service of the greatest and most munificent of lords. But that is not the right way to express it today.

Unhappily, no way has yet been found for a religion substantially to break with its past or modify its basic imagery.

The reason is that only one man in a million uses religious language in a first-hand way: the rest borrow old concepts. But now they borrow from a dead vocabulary, and this does harm. Can Christian language undergo a rebirth, or is the demand for a new body of fundamental images really a demand for a new religion?

7

THE UTILITY OF RELIGION

TOWARDS THE end of the eighteenth century two men independently reviewed the English scene. Each was a utilitarian, convinced that there was one scientific test by which all the prevailing beliefs, customs, and institutions, should be evaluated, namely, their tendency to promote human happiness. Utilitarianism represented, roughly speaking, the extension to the field of ethics of the Epicurean spirit which had lately triumphed in the physical sciences. But these two able men, both clear writers and liberal[1] spirits, reached opposite conclusions. As John Grote later remarked,[2] one must conclude that the utilitarian principle "does not furnish so unquestionable a test for settling differences of opinion as some of its advocates would make out".

The two men were Jeremy Bentham and William Paley. Paley's *Principles of Moral and Political Philosophy* appeared in 1785 and was an instant success. Paley was a theological utilitarian. He thought the business of life was the pursuit of happiness. Happiness consists in "the exercise of the social affections"; "the exercise of our faculties, either of body and mind, in the pursuit of some engaging end"; "the prudent constitution of the habits"; and health.[3] Now we need to discover a rule of life which will guide us to the happiness we desire. God discloses such a rule both through nature and scripture.[4] Virtue is "the doing good to mankind, in obedience to the will of God,

[1] Paley is sometimes pictured as an arch-conservative. But he took up the anti-slavery cause openly in 1788. *Works*, ed. A. Chalmers (1821), pp. xxxf.
[2] *An Examination of the Utilitarian Philosophy* (1870), p. 229.
[3] *Principles*, I, vi. To want of objects of affection "may be imputed the peevishness of monks"!
[4] II, iv.

and for the sake of everlasting happiness".[1] God is a benevolent creator, whose goodness is equally apparent in nature and in scripture. What he commands, what is in our interest, what nature teaches, and what is reasonable, all coincide. "So then actions are to be estimated by their tendency. Whatever is expedient, is right. It is the utility of any moral rule alone, which constitutes the obligation of it."[2]

Having established his theological utilitarianism, Paley outlines his moral and political philosophy. Reviewing the existing social institutions, including religion, he comes to a favourable verdict. They do on the whole satisfactorily promote human happiness. For example, habitual reverence towards God, developed by public worship, is "a considerable security against vice".[3]

It should be noticed that Paley does not regard God's commands as arbitrary. He does not reduce morality to fearful obeying of arbitrary decrees in order to avoid damnation. He thinks that by good probable arguments the truth of Christianity can be proved, and even that the divine benevolence can be proved by inspection of the natural order.[4] He does not agree that happiness is wrested, by human ingenuity, from a basically hostile world. He points to the artless happiness of children, shrimps, cats, and periwinkles. What he means is rather that "doing God's will" is the widest and most satisfactory expression of the moral criterion, which may *also* be expressed in other formulae such as "doing what tends to promote our own happiness", or "living according to nature", or "doing what tends to promote the public good". All coincide—they are like Kant's different formulations of the categorical imperative—but "doing the will of God" is the highest-level way of expressing the criterion of right action.

Accordingly, Paley regards the religious sanction as supplying the highest-level motive for doing good. Writers at that time distinguished different moral sanctions. There was the *natural*

[1] I, vii.
[2] II, vi.
[3] V, ix.
[4] *Principles*, II, v; cf. *Natural Theology* (1801), xxvi.

123

sanction of the pleasure and pain attached to prudent and im-
prudent conduct respectively. There was the *civil sanction*
provided by the law of the land. There was the sanction of public
opinion, called by Bentham the *moral or popular sanction*. And,
finally, there was the *religious sanction*, the fear of God's judgement. Paley thought this last sanction supremely important for
the common good. Secular utilitarians liked to say that the
natural, the civil, and the popular sanctions, would together
provide sufficient motive for people to do good, at least in a well-
ordered state. They were social reformers because they wanted
society to be changed into a more rationally-ordered one in
which these sanctions *would* be sufficient. Thus their reforming
impulse constituted an admission that these secular sanctions
are *not at present adequate* by themselves. So we may say that Paley
thinks that the *religious sanction* will make up for the observable
insufficiency of the other sanctions to make men virtuous
whereas the Benthamites think *social reform* will do so, and
regard the religious sanction as a proven failure.

Bentham's book was called *An Introduction to the Principles of
Morals and Legislation* and it finally appeared, after delays, in
1789. Bentham's utilitarianism is clearly in some ways stricter
and tougher-minded than Paley's. The Principle of Utility,
which in Paley summed up the essence of other criteria of
morality, in Bentham, is used simply to eliminate them as idle
verbiage.[1] We have no direct knowledge of what God's will may
be, only a host of divines telling us what they each think God's
will may be. The only sure way to know what God's will may be
is to determine with the help of the utility principle what is right
and what is wrong, and then assume that what is right is conformable to the will of God.[2] The inference is plain: talk of God's
will is simply redundant. Scientific ethics has no need of it. As
for a *sanction* to persuade people to be moral, the natural sanctions
of pleasure and pain are basically sufficient. They supply the
"groundwork" of the political and popular sanctions. The
religious sanction may be set aside. Insofar as God rewards or
punishes us in this life he does so by means of the natural sanc-

[1] See the long note to *Introduction*, II, xiv.
[2] *Introduction*, II, xviii.

tions; of what he may do in the next life we have no sure knowledge.[1]

Bentham's review of English institutions led him to see everywhere a need for urgent reform, and not least in the Church. But his express treatment of the problem of the utility of religion remains to this day little known, though it has been highly praised by John Stuart Mill[2] and Leslie Stephen.[3] It is a small book entitled *Analysis of the Influence of Natural Religion upon the Temporal Happiness of Mankind* (1822) by "Philip Beauchamp". This book was put together by the young George Grote (elder brother of John) out of a manuscript by Bentham which is now in the British Museum.

It has remained an obscure book for various reasons. Mrs. Grote, in her biography of her husband, concealed his part in it. Bentham's anti-Christian writings were left out of the complete edition of his works published by Bowring. The Benthamites were slow to break openly with the Church, and only did so, about 1810, over the issue of popular education. They preferred not to go to prison, like Richard Carlile, and tended to be discreet.[4] So "Philip Beauchamp" remained unacknowledged and obscure. Grote reprinted him privately in 1866, and "a new edition" was published by Truelove, a freethought publisher, in 1875. I quote from this last edition of what is now a scarce book.

Before summarizing Philip Beauchamp, let us recall what the main issues were. The orthodox were saying that religious belief is highly beneficial, both to the individual believer, and to the society in which it is established. Society needs religion, and is weakened by assaults on its religion. The public-spirited sceptic ought at the very least to keep his doubts to himself and not advertise them.

Mill says that only people who are already more than half sceptics will wish to invoke this argument. He thinks that the

---

[1] III.

[2] In his essay *The Utility of Religion* (1874), the second of three posthumously published essays on religion. I cite this essay often in what follows, but do not give page references because it is short and several editions are now readily available.

[3] *The English Utilitarians* (1900), Vol. II, pp. 338–61.

[4] See E. Halévy, *The Growth of Philosophic Radicalism* (E.T. 1928), pp. 282 96.

question of the utility of religion only becomes important when men are agreed that the question of its truth cannot be settled. If we knew it to be true its utility would be obvious. Talk of the utility of religion is heard in a period of religious decline. For example, most parents, although not Christians themselves, are glad for their children to have *some* religious education, though not too much. It is good educationally to have suffered some slight exposure to Christianity, if only to assist the appreciation of the arts and literature.

However, I think we can raise the discussion to a rather less ignoble level than that. In a company which includes Christians and non-Christians, the argument might be used by way of seeking common ground. A Christian might candidly say: "I believe Christianity to be true and I hope you will tolerate it because it has been and is beneficial. It has helped to hold society together, it has led men to lead good lives, there is a poetry and a beauty in it." These are not good reasons for believing, but they might be good reasons for tolerating Christianity, and perhaps even tolerating its continued establishment in a basically secular society.

The older social defence of religion, however, was pitched more strongly than this. It was claimed that the religious sanction is necessary to the social good. There were various strands in this claim.

The *first* is the claim that it is religion which teaches men their duty. This claim could have a merely factual meaning. Religious agencies are in fact in possession of the field: they are responsible for most of the moral education of the populace. If this is merely a contingent matter, then it can be changed, and the moral education of the people could be transferred to other agencies, as Mill pointed out. The historic association of the Church with the task is accidental and therefore variable.

But this claim could bear a stronger interpretation. It is religion which teaches men their duty, because our duty just is what God commands. Paley held this, though *not* in the highly vulnerable sense which so many philosophers have criticized.[1]

The *second* strand in the social defence of religion is the claim

---

[1] C. S. Lewis, in *The Problem of Pain* (1940), Chapter VI, did Paley a serious injustice on this point.

that religion not only best teaches men their duty, but that it is also uniquely effective in persuading them actually to *do* it. Religion is not only a teacher of morals, but also the best enforcer of morals. The fear of God's all-seeing eye and capacious memory, and the hope of winning his favour, are the strongest inducements to right conduct.

The *third* strand is the claim that religion's influence upon the moral life is more comprehensive than any other. There are important areas of the moral life upon which sanctions other than religion cannot be brought to bear effectively. The popular sanction may induce an outward conformity, but is unlikely to change the heart. The civil magistrate may be able to frame legislation which will stop me defrauding you, but he cannot make laws which will impel me to love you. Only religion can touch the whole of the moral life.

These arguments for the moral necessity of religion were central to the older debate. Others were used. For example, it was widely believed that atheists must suffer from despair, especially as death approached them. And, as the nineteenth century advanced, other arguments were brought in: we shall notice one or two examples later on. The Benthamites had thought that religion could simply be extinguished, without any replacement for it being needed. It simply did no worthwhile job at all. But the later nineteenth century was religious enough to feel that Christianity would have to be replaced by something else. Schopenhauer would replace it with true Metaphysics,[1] John Stuart Mill would replace it with the Religion of Humanity,[2] Freud would replace it with Science.[3] All allowed that traditional religion *had* played a useful part in the development of civilization: but it was now superseded and had become a harmful influence. It needed to be replaced by something which would do its job better. In a way, then, these very diverse men, Mill, Schopenhauer and Freud, all agreed that religion had a social function. They simply wished to replace an outmoded religion, Christianity, with a more up-to-date one.

[1] See the dialogue "On Religion" in *Parerga und Paralipomena* (1851).
[2] *The Utility of Religion.*
[3] *The Future of an Illusion* (ET, 1928), IX and X.

Philip Beauchamp was more radical. Like Russell,[1] he thought religion was all folly and deceit, and hoped it would soon disappear.

Two weaknesses in Paley's position were particularly apparent. Paley says *both* that obligatoriness means utility *and* that obligatoriness is a violent inducement resulting from the command of God, to which rewards and punishments are annexed. He holds that what is God's will for us, and what is in our own interest, coincide. To make this opinion reasonable and morally tolerable he must prove the divine benevolence, not only from revelation, but also from nature. He must show that it is a fact that God wills the happiness of his creatures. Nature, for Paley, has a smiling face: he is an optimist.

Philip Beauchamp breaks this up. For him, nature is harsh. Her "standing provisions" are pain, want, and uneasiness. The satisfaction of wants, the diminution of pain and unease, and the procuring of pleasure, depend entirely upon human skill.[2] If we met some new kind of berry, it would be folly to argue *a priori* that (because God is benevolent) the berry will turn out to be sweet-tasting and nourishing.[3] Our beliefs ought to be based upon experience and reason. Religion causes great harm by encouraging "extra-experimental belief": for by so doing it is infallibly the enemy of progress.

A second awkwardness in Paley's position is of a humorous kind. All his life he had difficulty with the doctrine of eternal punishment, although of course, it was not in his *own* interest to voice doubts on the matter! He might argue that the *belief* has morally beneficial results, by frightening men into virtue: but it is hard to see the utility of the *fact*. Hell is rather like the nuclear deterrent, which is only morally tolerable so long as the great Powers are frightened by it into keeping the peace. Its *use* would be intolerable. But the deterrent must be *credible*: it will only deter while the Powers seriously fear that it *may* be used. Similarly, a demythologized Hell will not frighten people into virtue. The deterrent has lost its credibility, and this is what has actually

---

[1] *Why I am not a Christian* (1957), nos. 1, 2 and 14.
[2] Beauchamp, p. 14. See also p. 12.
[3] p. 18.

happened in the last century. People don't believe in Hell any more. The compromise—Hell is a real possibility, but there is no one in fact in it—is unstable and ineffectual.

So Paley was in difficulty over Hell.[1] Beauchamp denies that it is a good deterrent even where it is sincerely believed.[2] If a penal system is to be efficacious, punishment must be administered promptly, and certainly, and must be moderate in its duration and intensity. God's punishments are remote and uncertain. They make up for this weakness by being, it is alleged, infinitely prolonged and intense. But this still further weakens their efficacy. They are either disregarded as preposterous by healthy men, or drive dying men into desperation and madness.[3]

When the emphasis is laid upon God's purpose of terrifying us into submission, Beauchamp has no difficulty in showing how nightmarish a picture of God is created. He begins by defining religion as "the belief in the existence of an almighty Being, by whom pains and pleasures will be dispensed to mankind, during an infinite and future state of existence", and his purpose is to ascertain whether such a belief is useful to mankind.[4] His emphasis upon Natural Religion is partly a stratagem to evade the accusation of blasphemy against what will follow, and partly because he wishes to criticize religions other than Christianity. We may think his definition of religion odd, but it is worth recalling that the belief in judgement and hell is perhaps the most nearly universal of religious beliefs[5]—a discouraging thought.

Now, says Beauchamp, if sincerely believed, a posthumous existence "is most likely to appear replete with pain and misery. The demonstration is brief and decisive."[6] "It is only to knowledge that we owe our respite from incessant pain and suffering"; where it fails "ignorance must generate incessant alarm and uneasiness". We are happy when we can predict the future

---

[1] See Chalmers' *Memoirs of Paley*, cited above, pp. vi–ix; and Paley's *Sermons on Several Subjects*, no. XXXI.

[2] Beauchamp, pp. 84ff.

[3] Beauchamp, pp. 46–52. For Hume on the efficacy of the religious sanction, see his *Dialogues* (Kemp Smith edition), pp. 219–226.

[4] Beauchamp, pp. 10, 11.

[5] S. G. F. Brandon, *The Judgement of the Dead* (1968), *passim*.

[6] Beauchamp, p. 12.

and secure ourselves against it; where we cannot, the future is full of terrors. The only straw we have to grasp at is the imagined character of God.[1] But the basic things which religion says about God are that he is possessed of limitless power and that this power is exercised in ways we cannot comprehend.[2] We must therefore picture him as a terrifying and capricious despot, the kind of sovereign whose favours are still more intimidating than his threats. The capricious mixture of good and evil in the world is conformable to this picture, though you could also hold, with Plato, that a good God struggles with intractable material, or, for that matter, that a malevolent God struggles to corrupt intractably good material.[3]

If the latent content of mankind's idea of God is always a terrifying and capricious despotism, why is its manifest content the opposite? Why must the Deity always be addressed in the language of the most devoted reverence and eulogy? Because we cannot punish omnipotence; our only method of influencing him is by heaping upon him the extravagant praise that despots love above all else.[4] The all-seeing eye of Omnipotence, a "universal espionage", ensures for him universal praise.[5]

Such a deity will approve most heartily of the priests who strengthen his dominion, and the ascetics, whose abasement witnesses to it. He cannot be sincerely believed to have an interest in making men happier or elevating their status.[6] His greatest wrath is reserved for those who presume to call in question his existence, "an affront of peculiar poignancy, to which the material despot is not exposed".[7] At bottom, for Beauchamp, religion is the worship of unlimited power, and experience teaches that power is used beneficently only where it is limited.[8]

Yet the sources of pleasure and pain would remain the same did this belief not exist. If virtuous conduct is temporally bene-

[1] Beauchamp, pp. 19, 20.
[2] 21, 22.
[3] 24n.
[4] Beauchamp, pp. 24ff. Compare Hume's *Natural History of Religion* (ed. H. E. Root, 1956), p. 67.
[5] Beauchamp, p. 40.
[6] 32ff.
[7] 34.
[8] 35–36.

ficial then men have the same motives to virtue whether they believe in six gods or none. So right conduct is everywhere the same; and what really distinguishes the religions from each other is the interest of each in its own peculiar cult. The very rise of religious toleration in modern society shows that differences of religious belief, and even its total absence, are no longer thought to be a matter of moral importance.[1] The inducements of religion are much less effective than is commonly claimed,[2] probably do more harm than good,[3] and owe most of their influence to the pressure of public opinion.[4] Without the support of public opinion, they avail very little.[5]

Beauchamp then proceeds to catalogue the mischiefs done by religious belief, first to the individual, and then to society.

Religion inflicts unprofitable suffering on the individual by persuading him that the supreme measure of his devotion is his readiness to suffer pain.[6] It imposes useless privations, such as fasting and celibacy.[7] It impresses upon his mind terrors which drive some even to madness, and it puts a tax on pleasure "by the infusion of preliminary scruples and subsequent remorse".[8]

The social mischiefs done by religion are equally grave. It creates factitious antipathies. Men are ready enough to hate each other without religion: but religion gives them a principle to hate each other upon with a clear conscience.[9] This irrational blame corrupts public morality.[10] Efforts to augment human happiness by an improved knowledge of facts are stigmatized as "unnatural". There was a time when religion was arrayed to prohibit "medicinal improvements" as "unnatural", but Beauchamp, too generously, thinks it now past![11]

[1] Beauchamp, pp. 37–42.
[2] 43–46.
[3] 46–52.
[4] 53–56.
[5] 56–62.
[6] 64.
[7] 65–67.
[8] 67–69.
[9] 69–76.
[10] 76–80.
[11] 83.

The most general intellectual damage done by religion is its tendency to disjoin belief from experience.[1] The basic theological beliefs are extra-experimental in themselves, but more than that, belief that a supernatural agent may intervene unpredictably in this world's affairs must tend to "dethrone and cancel the authority of experience in every instance whatever".[2] Once you admit extra-experimental beliefs, all the rules of evidence are subverted, as a flawless alibi was no defence against a charge of witchcraft. Belief in superhuman interference led the courts in the past to rely upon trial by ordeal rather than upon the weighing of evidence in the light of experience; and, if taken seriously, might lead men to pray for food rather than to labour for it.[3]

The mischief is further compounded when religion, seeking to verify itself, declares faith to be a virtue, and rewards it: so in effect attaching a premium to hypocrisy or credulity.[4] In one way and another men's ability to be kind to each other is actually impaired by religion. Its obscurities, its terrors, and its stringent requirements, reduce the believer to "a perpetual uneasiness and dissatisfaction with himself", "a sense of infirmity of purpose and dereliction of principle", a "feeling of inferiority and degradation". "A mind thus at variance with itself can never be at peace with anybody else, or feel sufficient leisure to sympathize with the emotions of others. It shelters its own vacillation under a plea of the general debasement and original wickedness of the whole human race" . . . a plea which encourages the believer to be as hard on others as he is upon himself.[5]

Beauchamp says at this point that "it is useless to affirm that religion does not in fact produce this unhappy result". That is because its influence is weak: but where its influence is strong, it does indeed tend to produce such a character—and he instances a Spanish monastery.[6] We are struck by the

[1] Beauchamp, pp. 84ff.
[2] 89.
[3] 91–97.
[4] 97–100.
[5] 101ff.
[6] 102f.

132

apriorism of Beauchamp's method: "Bentham's dialectic has always the same nature: it borrows as few elements as possible from empirical observation . . . He defines religion *a priori*, and looks for the necessary consequences of religion as so defined."[1] What he produces is a vivid version of a standard stereotype of the Christian believer as a man inwardly divided, cowed, self-hating and censorious. The stereotype is roughly the same as the popular Christian stereotype of the Pharisee, and so constitutes a kind of poetic revenge, one injustice being requited by another. In anti-Christian literature it appears in the eighteenth century and continues much the same in Nietzsche, in Freud, and in a great deal of modern fiction, both good (D. H. Lawrence) and bad (W. Somerset Maugham).

The remainder of Beauchamp's book is devoted to an anti-clerical diatribe which is highly entertaining, but is not particularly germane to our present purpose. Enough has been said to show that his work is more than a good period piece. It raises a number of interesting questions, and shows that the English utilitarians are not as destitute of psychological insight as is sometimes thought.[2]

Given the sort of utilitarianism from which both Paley and Beauchamp begin, it is inevitable that Beauchamp should have the better of the argument. For they both reckon that we know prior to religion what is right and what is wrong. What job is there, then, for religion to do in the field of morality? The suggestion is that it furnishes an extrapowerful sanction or inducement to do what is right. But *ex hypothesi* a utilitarian ethic needs no such extraneous sanction, for we have already created the strongest possible sanction by defining right conduct as that conduct which is in our interest. So it would seem that so far as this life is concerned Christianity can add nothing: a Christian utilitarian is simply a utilitarian carrying a good deal

---

[1] Halévy, *op. cit.*, p. 292.

[2] A good modern statement of the case against religion is M. R. Cohen, "The Dark Side of Religion" in *Religion Today, A Challenging Enigma*, ed. A. L. Swift Jr. (1933); repr. in *The Faith of a Liberal* (1946); and in Walter Kaufmann, *Religion from Tolstoy to Camus* (Harper Torchbook, 1964). Cohen's article uses many of the same arguments, and so shows Beauchamp's continuing relevance.

of excess baggage which he would be better without. It might seem then that Christian utilitarians will fall back upon the claim that Christianity is calculated to secure our eternal happiness. But by what standard will God assess us at the Last Judgement? If the standard by which we are to be judged is purely moral, and is to be applied to our past performance, then the secular utilitarian can be at no disadvantage compared with the Christian. On the other hand, if the Last Judgement is not by works alone, and God will examine us by some non-moral criteria, then the Christian is open to moral criticism. The secular utilitarian devotes his life to doing good, whereas the Christian utilitarian devotes his life partly to doing good and partly to performing those acts and developing those qualities which will help him to survive the Last Judgement. In that case it is admitted that Christianity is not a purely moral religion and some at least of its observances are open to criticism as immoral. So Beauchamp must get the better of the argument. The orthodox establishment men had chosen to fight on the wrong ground, and so were soundly beaten.

We could make a distinction here between two types of theology, which we might term *supplementary* and *transformative*. Paley's theology was supplementary. He did not seek to *transform* the prevailing system of thought but merely to draw from it a few additional corollaries, using its own conclusions and methods of argument.[1] Paley's theology was built upon the appeal to experience, the allegedly "Baconian" inductive method, and utilitarian ethics. He did not question any of these: he proposed to use them to establish the existence and goodness of God, and the truth of Christianity, by the same sort of arguments which would be used to establish the existence of the planet Neptune, or the character of Julius Caesar. Religious knowledge was a kind of supplement to secular knowledge, of the same kind and established by the same methods. But as such it was unexpectedly vulnerable. Beauchamp denies the soundness of the arguments purporting to establish it,[2] and attacks it as useless to morality.

[1] See Leslie Stephen's discussion, cited above.
[2] Beauchamp, pp. 87f.

I suspect that a sound theology must be *transformative*: it must do justice to the way in which the entry into religion transforms a man's entire way of looking at the world. The main business of religion is precisely this transformation. As an optional supplement to a basically secular outlook religion makes no sense. It is a standing temptation of liberal theologians to devise merely supplementary theologies.

But, and equally, it is because Beauchamp also sees religion only in the light of an optional supplement that he so obviously and repeatedly misses the point. Religion is something to be judged by the Principle of Utility: but Beauchamp cannot apprehend what religion is until he sees it as possibly judging and overthrowing that principle itself. You are quite simply not talking about religion at all until you are apprehending it as a force which might overthrow your entire system of thought.

The utilitarian measures religion by its utility: that is, he imagines that Christians and other religious believers must claim that observable temporal benefits will accrue to the individual and to society as a direct result of their religious profession. But I am not sure how far theologians have ever actually claimed this. I can think of only two classes of people who have said something of the kind. The first is a certain kind of Puritan or sub-puritan. Some puritans held that success in temporal enterprises, and conspicuous virtue, were criteria of election. This was called the "testimony of works". An authority on Calvin, however, describes this tendency as "contrary to authentic Calvinist thought".[1] I was once foolish enough to go to see a Billy Graham film in which a man was converted and promptly obtained a rise in salary. I thought it was ridiculous, and so do you.

The other class of people who have urged the temporal benefits conferred by religion have been certain apologists of established Churches. I believe they have misdescribed the situation, and I will try to explain how.

The French film director Louis Malle has recently paid a lengthy visit to India, and made there eight documentary films. Malle is very much a Frenchman of his time: perceptive,

[1] Theodore Wendel, *Calvin* (Collins: Fontana 1965), p. 277.

politically of the Left, and secular in outlook. In South India, everything morally objectionable in religion is glaringly apparent: the caste system, *real* sacred cows, the preposterously burgeoning superstition, disdainful priests battening on the woeful superstitions of the mob, self-torturing ascetics, a riot of nonsense. Obviously Malle saw it through Marxist eyes, and obviously it is indefensible. You could not use in such a context the arguments by which a headmaster might defend compulsory Chapel. It was so grotesque that Malle stayed to watch and to film, and slowly felt his mind change. It is difficult to express what he came to feel except in the most wretched clichés. He says something to the effect that industrial civilization is breaking up in boredom and internal conflicts caused by spiritual *anomie*, whereas in India religion offers some real resistance to social disintegration. One might compare the situation of old people in the two cultures: contrast an old man in North Europe with an old Indian, with his loincloth, beard and fierce eyes, chanting the Upanishads before a South Indian shrine. It is the latter who is *interesting*. Alas, these are clichés, but the right way to begin a sentence about religion is not "Because religion confers so many benefits upon society, keeping the crime rate down and recalling the wicked to the path of virtue . . . and so forth", but "In the world you will have tribulation; but be of good cheer", or "In spite of everything that can and should be said against religion, *nevertheless* . . ."

The best Christian theologians and writers have not in fact been particularly concerned to stress the temporal utility of religion. They have talked of temptations and afflictions, and of the faith and hope whereby these may be surmounted. They have held that the consolations of religion are not observable benefits, come only occasionally, and are neither to be sought nor to be relied upon. Philip Beauchamp says that "in estimating the chances of life and death, of health and disease, no insurer ever inquires whether the actions of the applicant have been agreeable or disagreeable to the Deity":[1] but I doubt whether Beauchamp could produce any statement by a reputable theo-

[1] Beauchamp, p. 20.

logian claiming that the actuarial statistics of believers differ from those of unbelievers.

But I do not think it follows that religion is simply redundant, and the arguments which propose to prove as much are less strong than is often thought. John Stuart Mill, for example, argues that, although humanity is certainly greatly indebted to Jesus, his recorded teaching ought not to be canonized *en bloc*. In the Gospels, what is noble lies side by side with much baser metal. Since the Churches canonize the whole, both good and bad, Jesus' best teaching can only produce its best moral effects in the lives of Christians if they are guilty of a certain dishonesty in regard to the sacred text, selecting what is best while professing to follow the whole. Mill therefore argues that the morally earnest unbeliever, who learns from Jesus without making a god of his teacher, is in the better position. Like Schopenhauer and Freud, Mill suggests that what is good in Christianity is too much distorted and corrupted by the setting in which it is presented to us. And he believes that the best things which Jesus taught now live on, independent of the authority of their original teacher, and are in no danger of being forgotten.

Here I hold that Mill is simply foolish. In our own chastened century we have learned of what those whom he calls "the best and foremost portion of our species" are capable. It is not yet, and never will be, time to dismiss the teacher because we have reached heights of "improvement" from which we cannot fall. And I do not think it dishonest to select from Scripture. Mill knew little of Biblical criticism.

I also wish to criticize an argument of Freud. Freud says that religion provides man with an *affective* basis for his allegiance to culture, whereas science provides him with a *rational* basis.[1] It is of course important to Freud that cultural laws be obeyed. But when cultural laws are backed by religion they are made vulnerable to sceptical attacks on religion. It is true, he says, that by declaring that God forbids murder "we invest the cultural prohibition with a quite peculiar solemnity, but at the same time we risk making its observance

[1] *The Future of an Illusion*, p. 80.

dependent upon belief in God".[1] It would be better "to leave God out of the question altogether and admit honestly the purely human origin of all cultural laws and institutions. . . . Men would (then) realize that these (rules) have been made, not so much to rule them, as, on the contrary, to serve their interests".[2] And in the long run culture would be stronger for the change.

I don't think Freud sees it quite correctly. Let me take the example of monogamy. In many countries nowadays you can marry either by civil ceremony alone or by civil ceremony and with religious rites. Now it seems to me that monogamy is obviously the best arrangement for regulating the intercourse of the sexes. I do not propose to argue this at length, but will only say that there need be no theological premisses in the argument. All consideration of fashionable follies and hard cases gives place to the fact that the great mass of mankind like monogamy. So monogamy is a clear case of a moral institution which is not in need of the religious sanction to prop it up. It stands perfectly well upon its own feet. It is in our interest to abide by it. It is seemingly a clear case of what Bentham would have called the redundancy of the religious sanction.

Yet equally obviously, where the culture allows people a free choice between civil marriage and marriage with religious rites, a large number of people voluntarily choose religious rites, including a great many who otherwise have little allegiance to religion.

The history of Christianity is particularly striking. As an apocalyptic religion, early Christianity had no particular interest in marriage. It merely acquiesced in the Roman practice. The first traces of Christian rites are found in the fourth century, but "it is not until the ninth century that we find a detailed account of nuptial ceremonies": and the order of proceeding is exactly that of the ancient pagan Roman *confarreatio*.[3] It was not until the Council of Trent that the

---

[1] *The Future of an Illusion*, pp. 71f.

[2] 73.

[3] T. A. Lacey, *Marriage in Church and State* (1947 edn.), pp. 41–42, quoting the *Responsa ad Bulgaros* of Nicholas I.

Western Church declared that the use of Christian rites was essential to a valid marriage.

So, contrary to what Freud suggests, marriage (in Christendom at least) began as a purely natural institution. It was first deemed a sacrament by Hincmar of Reims in the ninth century.[1] Only very gradually was marriage religiously reinforced or sacralized by the Church. The religious solemnization of marriages is to this day in many countries more a matter of popular demand than of clerical imposition. And in Christianity the sacralization of marriage is a secondary development.

Philip Beauchamp suggests that religious bodies wax most vehement about matters of cultic observance. This has happened. Churches have fought over the use of leavened bread in the eucharist, and the way the sign of the cross is made. But no one in Christianity or out of it regards such disputes as particularly edifying. Both within Christianity and outside it people are most impressed by the Church's resistance to tyranny and injustice and its energy in the relief of suffering. It is striking that the witness is most moving and telling in precisely the areas whose morality is most obvious— the very areas which seem to stand in the least need of religious reinforcement.

For example, John Leonard Wilson was Bishop of Singapore in 1942 when that territory was overrun by the Japanese. For a time he was immured in the notorious Changi Jail. There he endured torture, refused to betray his friends or renounce his faith, and strove to keep up the morale of his fellow prisoners. After the war was over he received one of his gaolers into the Church.

Now there is nothing peculiarly Christian about courage. The point of this example, and of the example of marriage, is that *religious "reinforcement" is most highly valued where it is seemingly least needed.* And that makes one feel that when Bentham says that the religious sanction is redundant, or when

---

[1] Augustine used the term "sacrament", but probably only in a non-technical sense, as meaning "contract" or "covenant": See Willy Rordorf's article, previously cited, in the *Journal of Ecclesiastical History*, XX, p. 210.

Freud says that though it was once powerful it ought now to be abandoned, they have missed the point. There are certain great moments when what is central in religion and what is most precious in morality coincide—Francis kisses the leper, Luther takes his stand, Gandhi touches the untouchables, a bishop endures torture, a couple exchange vows—and such moments are of a worth which makes the criticisms of Bentham and Freud seem idle. These are all occasions whose morality is perfectly obvious to all men and does not need external reinforcement, but to say that and only that is foolish: rather as it would be foolish to say that, since that we all know that jealousy is a bad thing, Shakespeare's *Othello* has nothing to teach us.

Having said so much in criticism of Philip Beauchamp let us end by saying where he and his successors are right. A great deal of historic Christianity has been gloomy and careworn. Even the eucharistic liturgy has resounded with cries for mercy and professions of unworthiness. In many north European countries the emphasis upon "Worthy Communion" between the seventeenth and nineteenth centuries was so strong as nearly to extinguish the practice of communicating.[1] People have been overburdened with religious anxiety and scruples to the point where they have been trapped by religion rather than released by it. There is some justice in the standard literary stereotype of the Christian, and once Christianity has suffered this kind of psychological corruption it is very difficult to shake it off.

[1] Jeremy Taylor, *The Worthy Communicant* (1660), is a fairly moderate example. He is a humane man, and counsels frequent communion. But he surrounds the act of communicating with a baroque elaboration of what look all too like *precautionary* measures. The sacred is becoming alien and dangerous.

8

THE CASE AGAINST THEOLOGY

CRITICISM OF theology as an intellectual enterprise is so widespread that the word itself, and many other words associated with it, have acquired in common speech pejorative overtones. One thinks of terms like *theological* (trivial, hair-splitting), *dogmatic* (rigid, closed), *propaganda*, *indoctrination* (manipulation), *orthodoxy* (unthinking conformity) and *doctrinaire*. The case against theology has been so readily and widely accepted that the time has come to ask precisely what it is, and how strong it is.

The objections to theology may be thought to be *intellectual* objections rather than *moral* objections, and indeed the Christian tradition itself used to distinguish the intellectual virtues (of sanity, wit, wisdom, prudence, and artistry) from the specifically moral virtues. However, critics impute to the theologians sins against the intellectual light of such gravity that their criticisms can only be called moral criticisms. If a theologian is charged with lacking moral seriousness, with partiality, with disingenuousness in his arguments—or, more briefly, double-speak —then these charges amount to *moral* criticisms.

So I shall describe a number of charges which have been made against theology. There are two main areas in which one might search for material: one is the Renaissance revolt against scholasticism, and the other the period since Kant. I decided against the former, as being mainly of historical interest; but the latter turns out to be very interesting. I do not mean that every important critique of theology made since Kant has been made directly under his influence. Matthew Arnold attacks theologians and popular theologies in *St. Paul and Protestantism* (1870) and his subsequent religious writings; and Tolstoy wrote a large *Criticism of Dogmatic Theology* (c. 1880, published 1891, 1903).[1] Neither Arnold nor Tolstoy can be called a close and exact student of Kant: but the way they wrote does belong to the post-Kantian period in a recognizable sense.

The first problem is one of definition. What is theology? The critics allow that what passes under that name "includes a lot of perfectly good science which is not theory of god",[2] such as historical, textual and linguistic studies. Nor is it writing about religion which makes a man a theologian, for we would not readily call Freud or Hobbes theologians, though both wrote much about religion. What makes a man a theologian, it is said, is that he expounds the beliefs of a religious community, to which he himself belongs, in a particular way—a persuasive way. So the critics' heaviest fire is directed against systematic or dogmatic theology of a confessional kind.

Walter Kaufmann[3] argues as follows: the Oxford English Dictionary defines theology as "the study or science which treats of God, His nature and attributes, and His relations with man and the universe", and it goes on to say that there are two sorts of theology: "*Dogmatic theology*, theology as authoritatively held and taught by the church; a scientific statement of Christian dogma", and "*Natural theology*, theology based upon reasoning from natural facts apart from revelation". Natural theology might claim to be a respectable science: but, says Kaufmann, it is for good reasons largely discredited or abandoned today. And even if it were permissible to infer something supra-natural from natural facts, it is not the facts alone which determine what is invoked at this point, but some preconceived ideas derived from a particular religion. "*At the crucial point, natural theology falls back on dogmatic theology.*" So, for Kaufmann, theology's weakness is the consequence of the collapse of Natural Theology, and with it of the linking arguments which used to make a bridge between Natural Theology

---

[1] For an account of this book see Aylmer Maude's *Life of Tolstoy: Later Years* (1910).

[2] Richard Robinson, *An Atheist's Values* (1964), p. 116. Cf. Walter Kaufmann, *The Faith of a Heretic* (Anchor edition 1963) pp. 89ff., 132, (hereafter cited as "Kaufmann", with a page number).

[3] Kaufmann, 91f.

and Dogmatic Theology. And Dogmatic Theology is partisan: there are at least as many dogmatic theologies as there are Churches. Just as Troeltsch showed long ago that there is no single Christian social ethic, so there is no single Christian dogmatic theology—only the many theologies which different Churches have held in different periods. Kaufmann, like other writers, thinks empirical religious studies to be of great value and importance. But he thinks that they are corrupted if they are organized in a faculty of theology in a way that implies that dogmatic theology is the master and they are servants. Where this is the case an extra-academic interest, that of some church or group of churches, is really dictating the syllabus of studies, and even the conclusions to be reached.

So the critic defines theology as being, roughly, what a traditional Roman Catholic would call "dogmatic theology" or what Karl Barth called "Church Dogmatics". We can see in general what he means, but the matter is not quite as simple as that. For it might be retorted that British and American Faculties of Medicine are not (by parallel reasoning) academically respectable either. They serve what outside professional bodies, namely the B.M.A. and the A.M.A., decree to be medical orthodoxy, and do not give a fair hearing to medical heresies and medical paganisms. Scientology would be an example of a medical heresy, and African folk medicine, or traditional Chinese medicine, would be examples of medical paganism. It can be replied to this that Western medical research *is* willing to enquire whether African rituals do assuage mental pain and whether acupuncture really does help in rheumatic disorders. But theologians too can say that Christian theology has been receptive to influence from the study of comparative religion—for example in the *religionsgeschichtliches-chule*. And on the general point, theologians in German universities since Hegel have not exactly been slavishly bound by the official orthodoxy of the Churches. A stronger objection to the analogy is that Western Medicine is based upon the scientific method. It has no essential interest in maintaining an orthodoxy in defiance of well-established facts. If it nevertheless sometimes *appears* to do so, this is human weakness:

whereas a dogmatic theology has an *essential* interest in maintaining itself unchanged. A dogmatic theology binds together a Christian community and tells that community that it holds the same Faith as the first Christians, and this social function of dogma takes precedence over the claims of truth. It is in principle harder for a Reformed theologian to say "Calvin was wrong" or "St. Paul was wrong" than for a medical man to say "Fabricius was wrong" or "Galen was wrong", because the theological community is obliged to be true to its past in ways in which the medical community is not. So there remains, it may be said, something academically dubious about theology. We can smell out just the same thing very quickly in other contexts, for example in the early history of psychoanalysis. Freud was such a great man, and such a powerful personality, that it was difficult at first to discuss his ideas with due objectivity. To describe this feature of the psychoanalytic movement people employ religious metaphors, speaking of Freud's *disciples*, of psychoanalytic *orthodoxy*, and of *schisms* within the movement. Christian writers upon psychoanalysis have themselves been willing to use these metaphors, but their very aptness suggests a damaging criticism of theology. For the metaphors are considered apt insofar as the early psychoanalysts were *irrational* about their beliefs.

Marxism has had a similar history. If we read a Marxist we notice very quickly certain features of his method:

(1) He attempts to enlist distinguished support. For example, Tolstoy was a very great man. It would be impossible simply to eliminate him from Russian history. Therefore he must be shown to have been a virtual or implicit Marxist-Leninist, by appropriate exegesis of his writings.

(2) He uses a distinctive jargon. This jargon seems to be partly a badge of membership of his group, and partly to be intended to pull the wool over the reader's eyes. Often the jargon is badly dated and no longer fits the facts. For example, we hear about a character called a capitalist who owns and manages factories, though we know that nowadays the manager is a salaried employee; and the investor of capital

is, likely as not, a committee which manages a pension fund.

(3) He cites authorities to prove his own orthodoxy, as if the mere quotation of a few words from a letter by Lenin were enough to settle a question.

(4) He likes to use a form of *tu quoque* argument: "insofar as you are an honest and good man you cannot but be in agreement with me. Any alternative to my point of view would plunge you into such a sink of iniquity that I am sure that you are really of my party. If you love your fellow men and care for social justice you must be a marxist whether you admit it openly or not."

These four features of Marxist writing are precisely those which have led some people to call Marxism a religion, and many people to use metaphors drawn from theology in discussing Marxist writings. Once again, the use of these metaphors of *orthodoxy, schism, heresy, sacred writings, exegesis* and the like, implies a damaging criticism of theology. If it is intellectually a bad thing to cite proof-texts from the *Thoughts of Chairman Mao* then it would seem to be equally a bad thing to do so in the field from which the metaphor was drawn, namely Biblical exposition.

We can further elaborate the parallels. Anyone who develops a tradition, and tries to interpret it sympathetically to his own generation, is torn between conflicting loyalties. On the one hand, he has to placate conservatives by protesting that he is maintaining the tradition unchanged; but, on the other, he is trying to appeal to outsiders, by suggesting to them that the traditional doctrines are not really so unpalatable to them as they might suppose. Thus he is obliged to adopt a disingenuous and systematically ambiguous way of speaking which means one thing to one group and another thing to another. After generations of theorists have developed the tradition in this way a situation of total confusion is created, while it still continues to be asserted that the tradition remains unchanged. In time the tradition becomes so diverse, and the permissible gymnastics so contorted, that one suspects that a cunning man could use the accepted materials and methods to prove any opinion whatever.

Various examples are given of the alleged double-talk of theologians. Bultmann is reluctant to say categorically whether he believes in Hell or not.[1] Barth is reluctant to say definitely whether he believes in universal redemption or not. Yet surely it is a matter of great moral importance whether we believe in a God who will save all or a God who will save some and reject some. Ambiguity on this point seems to be caused by the quasi-political role of the theologian in relation to the church community. He has to placate both conservatives and liberals. But the ambiguity is damaging because it leaves us in doubt whether God loves all men or some men.

The use of "interpretation" to reconcile contrary statements is alleged also to be dishonest. For example, the Council of Trent stated that unbaptized infants, "be their parents Christian or infidel, are born to eternal misery and perdition". But the current Catholic teaching is that such infants, though admittedly deprived of supernatural beatitude,[2] will enjoy a state of perfect natural happiness. The theologian has a duty to "reconcile" these statements.

The result is very confusing. In the plain man's eyes the statements of the Second Vatican Council on such topics as religious liberty or the Jews contradict earlier official statements. But the earlier statements are not formally withdrawn. Do we conclude that the theologian has a duty to find a compromise formula somewhere in the middle or that he has a duty to interpret the earlier statement so as to bring it into line with the later? A suspicion could arise that the protestations of Vatican II about the Jews are not to be taken at face value. Perhaps they are over-corrections, intended at the time of utterance to be read in the light of earlier statements which are tacitly understood to remain authoritative?

Almost every lay critic of theology maintains that the Church teaches its doctrines in crude literal form to the masses, while simultaneously the theologians are explaining these same doctrines away for the benefit of more sophisticated people.

[1] Kaufmann, 96f.

[2] By omitting this qualifying clause, Kaufmann (p. 101), perhaps unintentionally, strengthens his own argument that there is a clear contradiction here.

The classical Christian doctrine about Easter and the Ascension is that at Easter the corpse of Jesus stirred, revived, stood up and walked, and forty days later flew up into the sky. Every medieval or Renaissance painting depicting these subjects testifies as much. The theologians, or many of them, no longer believe this, or appear no longer to believe it. If they no longer believe it, they are no longer Christians:[1] but they are reluctant to say openly and plainly what they think, for fear of alienating the mass of Church people. In the Preface to *Honest to God*, Dr. J. A. T. Robinson appeared to say that *both* the conservatives *and* the radical revisionists could be right.[2] A charge of theological opportunism might be brought here. People demand an ideology which will rationalize their prejudices and tell them that all is well with them. Thus, the religious book trade markets traditional theology for the consumption of conservative churchmen, and radical or liberal theology for the fellow-travellers. It is in nobody's interest that the two different products should come into conflict with each other, so a policy of live and let live prevails. But where in all this is heard the voice of truth?

Yet the accusations of disingenuousness sometimes seem to ring hollow. Tolstoy was a passionate moralist who in the Postscript to *The Kreutzer Sonata* went to the Kierkegaardian extreme of denouncing sexual love as egoistic and requiring the total renunciation of it.[3] On November 1, 1902, he completed his *Appeal to the Clergy*.[4] In this document he outlined what he took to be the popular orthodox theology of Christianity and attacked it as obviously false. For Tolstoy, the heart of Christianity was the Sermon on the Mount, but it seemed to him that, for the Church, it was a barbarous salvation-history which cannot be sincerely believed because it does not make sense. Popular orthodoxy is a tissue of absurdities and immoralities, and it has smothered and stifled the real message of the Gospel, which is disinterested love.

---

[1] Kaufmann, 124f.
[2] *Honest to God* (1963), pp. 8ff.
[3] His own practice was less strict, as Gorky tells.
[4] *Essays and Letters*, tr. Aylmer Maude (World's Classics, 1903), pp. 341ff.

Yet curiously enough Tolstoy himself, when purveying his teaching to peasants and children in the form of folk-tales, told stories in which angels and demons play an essential part in the plot.[1] Was he not committing precisely the same offence as that of the Church? If Tolstoy were taxed on this point his reply would be that one must speak to the peasants in language they understand. But the Church could say the same.

The absurdities of exegesis have often been denounced. In a famous letter to his patron, Can Grande della Scala, the poet Dante takes the verses "When Israel came out of Egypt and the House of Jacob from among a strange people, Judah was his sanctuary and Israel his dominion." Dante comments:

> If we regard *the letter alone* what is set before us is the exodus of the Children of Israel from Egypt in the days of Moses; if the *allegory*, our redemption wrought by Christ; if the *moral* sense, we are shown the conversion of the soul from the grief and wretchedness of sin to the state of grace; if the *anagogical*, we are shown the departure of the holy soul from the thraldom of this corruption to the liberty of eternal glory.[2]

The medieval assumption was that there was a *multiplex intelligential* in every line of Scripture, and Dante's own distinction of four levels of meaning derives from Aquinas. The exegesis of earlier periods is equally fanciful, if not always quite so systematically fanciful. Far-fetched exegesis is attributed by the Gospel-writers to Jesus and was practised by Paul. The rabbis were masters of it.[3]

I have two immediate comments to make upon this accusation. In the first place, the critic must beware of laying contradictory charges. It sounds as if theology is being accused both of rigidity and of waywardness. It is accused of rigidity in moving from infallible source-material to predetermined conclusions; and it is accused of waywardness in that it is permissible to read so much into the sources that

[1] See, for example, the stories in *Twenty-three Tales*, tr. Aylmer Maude (World's Classics).

[2] This translation taken from *The Divine Comedy: Hell*, tr. D. L. Sayers (Pelican, 1949), p. 15. The source is *Epistola X*, 140ff. See Dante's *Latin Works* (Temple Classics, 1904), pp. 347f.

[3] Examples in Kaufmann, pp. 105ff.

anything at all can be extracted from them. If a theologian is a traditionalist he will be criticized on the former count; if he is a revisionist he will be attacked on the latter count. The critic himself may become infected with the arbitrariness he denounced.

In the second place, the arbitrariness of exegesis may not matter quite so much as might be thought.[1] Three of the most valuable religious writers in the modern period have been Kierkegaard, Tolstoy, and Martin Buber. They were all men whose influence has been very much against any kind of speculative and systematic theology, but they themselves were all capable of approving exceedingly fanciful exegeses. Few preachers have got more out of a text than Kierkegaard, but the religious value of his writings is not particularly dependent upon the soundness of his exegesis. Tolstoy, in his *Union of the Four Gospels*, simply omitted what did not appeal to him, such as most of the miracles. Like many an English Victorian, he says that, at the Feeding of the Five Thousand, Jesus and his party shared out their own provisions and the rest of the crowd followed their example.[2] But, again, Tolstoy's writings are not shown to be worthless when his exegesis has been shown to be arbitrary.

Again, Martin Buber's *Tales of the Hasidim*[3] is by common consent one of the best of all religious books. The brief anecdotes by which the wisdom of rabbis is communicated to the reader often depend upon far-fetched points of exegesis— but it does not matter. The world of the Hasidic revival is full of the more unattractive features of religion—trances, ecstasies, superstition, bizarre beliefs—and so are the worlds of the *Golden Legend*, the *Philokalia*, and the *Paradise of the Fathers*. But it does not matter. If we can sort the wheat from the chaff in

[1] I do not mean that an exact and rigorous attempt to discover what we can about the message of Jeremiah is unimportant, but that religion has never been so closely and literally tied to its sacred texts as some people would like to pretend. Few, if any, theologies can make a serious claim to be based on rigorous exegesis of a sacred text.

[2] Maude's *Life* (cited above) II, p. 41.

[3] ET, Schocken Books, New York (1961). Definitive German edition, *Dei Erzählungen der Chassidim* (1949).

these cases, why may we not treat Calvin with the same indulgence?

Walter Kaufmann has an answer to this. He says that "with extremely few exceptions religion is most moving in the form of stories—stories that challenge the way we live". He says that this is true of the Old and New Testaments, as well as of Tolstoy and Buber. We might add to these the sardonic tales told by Kierkegaard, or the illustrations which make less intolerable the philosophical works of Jean-Paul Sartre. Few theologians can reach this level, says Kaufmann. "Most religious beliefs I should class with ritual: at best beautiful; more often, superstitious."[1]

So I suspect that the reason why Kaufmann cannot be as kind to Calvin as to the Hasidim is that, in Calvin, the scientific pretensions, the appearance of systematic completeness, the *dogma* are what is most prominent. Any religious wisdom in Calvin is concealed in the background. In the Hasidim, the apparatus of superstitious beliefs is relatively unobtrusive, it is in the background. The tales of the Hasidim are closer in spirit to the parables of Jesus. Calvin is a man who would dig the marginal details out of Jesus' parables—Abraham's bosom, and where the man with no wedding garment was thrown—make of them a system, and so altogether lose sight of the original religious point of the parable. It is the dogmatic theological urge in Calvin which leads him to obscure, or to miss the point of, what religion is all about.[2]

We now reach the heart of Kaufmann's charges against theology, which turn out to be charges against Christian theology in particular. The specifying differentia of Christianity is its theology. Christianity is an inescapably theological religion. (Islam is theological too, but its theology is much simpler.) Without its specific theology, Christianity is only a form of Unitarianism, or a Jewish sect. So in Christianity theology, dogmatic belief, is and has to be in the foreground.

---

[1] *Religion from Tolstoy to Camus* (1964 edn.), pp. 42f. Compare Matthew Arnold, *Literature and Dogma* (1873), for an interesting attack on dogmatic theologians for failing to understand what kind of book the Bible is, and treating it as if it were a kind of legal text rather than poetry.

[2] I do not say that this charge is just—only that it is made.

But the heart of religion is not in theology, and Christianity's theological itch, which has so dominated its history, is its undoing as a religion. For theology is a bogus science which cannot be made rigorous. Because it is tied to particular institutions it has helped to make Christianity fissiparous and factious. Kaufmann draws a practical conclusion: the theological seminaries "create many of the problems that their products are expected to resolve. . . . Having been trained to see Catholicism as the Catholics do not see it, Judaism as the Jews do not experience it . . . the young clergyman is expected to collaborate with priests and rabbis and to busy himself in the ecumenical movement, doing his best . . . to heal breaches which, but for the training he and the other ministers, rabbis, and priests, received, would long have disappeared."[1]

Kaufmann, then, argues that Christianity is an essentially *theological* religion, which only differentiated itself from Judaism by its dogmatic assertions about Jesus. To *break* with these assertions is to break with Christianity. But these assertions can only be *retained* at the price of some measure of intellectual dishonesty. To maintain today that these assertions are still in some sense true involves contemporary theologians in the sins of using deliberately ambiguous language, manipulating the evidence, and so on.

Kaufmann does not list the assertions, though the bodily Resurrection of Jesus from the grave would seem, for him, to be one of them. And here is a difficulty in his position: for theologies have been more diverse, and diverse in more ways, than he allows. As an illustration of diversity of *content* among theologians whose "orthodoxy" is generally accepted, one might contrast the treatment of Christ's incarnation, death, and Resurrection, by St. Paul and St. John, or by St. Athanasius and St. Anselm. As for diversity of *method*, it is clear that Schleiermacher, Calvin, and St. Thomas Aquinas have quite different ideas as to what theology is and how you set about doing it. Again, some forms of Christianity have been relatively indifferent to theology.

It is clear that a theologian works within a tradition, but it

[1] Kaufmann, p. 134.

is not clear that a tradition must be understood as a system of conclusions. It has been described as "a cluster of questions". Kaufmann imputes to the theologian a situation which the theologian himself does not experience, except in a few, admittedly bad, cases. Kaufmann appears to wish to criticize both the narrowness of the limits within which Roman Catholic theologians used to have to work *and* the comparative latitude which the German protestant theologian has enjoyed. He criticizes the former for being a party hack and the latter for having lost touch with the orthodox tradition altogether.

But we could use other analogies to illustrate the way a theologian feels about his work, and the intellectual limits within which he moves. An architect works within limitations: he can specify only materials which are actually available; the erection of his building must be technically feasible; his building must be one that his client likes, and is prepared to pay for; his building must be functional; and its design must be intelligible to the public who will be living with, seeing, and using the building. The limitations are considerable, and we recognize that to make beautiful buildings within these limits is not easy. An architect must be prepared to fight for his integrity as an artist, and must not sell out. When we look at an old building, in order to measure the achievement of its architect, we need to recall the cultural situation and the limits within which he worked. Occasionally it happens that a great architect finds a new way of solving an old architectural problem. He seems to transcend limits which his predecessors thought inescapable, and to change the way people feel about buildings. But some of the limitations under which architects work are relatively immutable. Facts about the dimensions and ergonomics of the human body, and facts about climate, light, and sound, determine that floors must support the body's weight, roofs must keep out rain, ceilings must be high enough for a man to stand, rooms must be illuminated, staircases must be climbable, and so forth. The limits are strict: but it is still possible to be creative within them.

T. S. Kuhn[1] has made a distinction between two kinds of

[1] *The Structure of Scientific Revolutions* (1962).

advance in scientific enquiry. There is the pursuit of research within a given framework of assumptions, and there is occasionally a revolutionary change in the assumptions. Most practitioners work within a given framework or style: a few creative minds open up quite new perspectives. Something of the kind happens in the arts, it happens in philosophy, and it can happen in theology too.

Now it happens in philosophy, in novel-writing, and in poetry that we do not regard a man as quite first-class unless he has something of the creative in him. A Kantian who is *just* a Kantian is not quite a philosopher. A man must if he can find his own voice. And the same is true in theology: a theologian whose opinions are simply identical with those of his master is not a theologian. There have been periods when theology was very like the law, and when a man who sought a theological opinion hoped to get advice which was as impersonal and objective as a good legal opinion. But these periods are not generally reckoned great creative periods, and should not be regarded as typical of theology at its best or even its strongest. In the modern period it has been highly diverse.

Kaufmann suggests that Christianity from the first stood or fell with certain bald dogmatic assertions, and one of them he takes to be the bodily Resurrection of Jesus. But the New Testament writers themselves give testimony on the subject which is much more varied than Kaufmann supposes. Kaufmann supposes that he can frame a proposition about the Resurrection of Jesus which is clear in meaning—that is, can mean only one thing—and to which every theologian who can properly be called a Christian must assent. His whole case against theology depends upon this supposition: and it is false.[1] Right from the beginning Christianity has been more diverse than people think: there never was, and never could be, one and only one orthodox set of beliefs.

Like many other critics, Kaufmann supposes that a theologian is set by his Church a system of conclusions to be reached, a body

[1] See, for example, "Easter: A Statement", by G. W. H. Lampe, in Lampe and D. M. MacKinnon, *The Resurrection* (1966).

of materials from which to begin, and maybe a method by which to work. He might also be free to choose between, say, a Thomist and a Kantian philosophical frame within which to work. And of course the answer is that doing theology simply does not feel like that, and that the great theologians differ from each other in the same sort of ways that the great philosophers differ from each other. It would be hard to name a good theologian who really looks as if he is fabricating arguments in support of foregone conclusions. Certainly great theologians have perpetrated bad arguments: but so have great philosophers.

People may object to the comparison, because some philosophers and some theologians in modern times have been anxious to dissociate their subjects from each other. But this is an aberration, and a very unscholarly one. Many, perhaps most, of the great philosophers of the past wrote extensively about religion.

No one would wish to deny that there have been aberrations, sterile periods, and follies in the history of theology: but our present question is whether the enterprise of theology *as such* is misguided and must be intellectually objectionable. That is not proven.

But two serious objections do remain. The first is that no actual Church has yet solved the problem of doctrinal evolution. Churches are hoarders, very bad at pruning out and discarding obsolete elements: or they are perhaps like coral reefs which grow by gradual accretion. There are numerous time-honoured popular Christian beliefs which are almost certainly false, superstitious, and harmful. Belief in evil spirits is one of them. Some of these beliefs have in addition played a large part in theology. The belief in the virginal conception of Jesus by Mary is an example. We may think this belief to be of mythological origin, we may suppose that its rise was associated with mistranslation into Greek of an Old Testament text such as Isaiah 7:14. But however the belief arose it has done great harm. It has suggested that Jesus was not an ordinary man, it has helped to poison people's feelings about the process of reproduction, and it has encouraged ugly and useless forms of asceticism.

So the belief ought to be abandoned. But there is at present no likelihood of this at all, even though everyone knows that Christian language and devotion are extensively impregnated with absurd and offensive beliefs. No one knows how to be rid of them.

But at least we would make a beginning if theologians—and by that I mean every thinking Christian with a concern for truth—were less tolerant of the obscurantism and intellectual permissiveness of a good deal of Church life. In famous historical cases like those of Galileo and Darwin, the Church authorities have been rightly blamed for wishing to shelter the simple faithful from the impact of new ideas. Nowadays, Christian intellectuals can make the same mistake out of a desire not to seem arrogant, not to risk dividing the Church, not to criticize language and practices which are felt to be edifying, even if not to be taken at face value. But this spirit of toleration over the years slowly erodes the Church's intellectual self-respect. And, nowadays, religious intellectuals no longer speak a learned language: they speak in the vernacular, and the man in the street overhears what they are saying. He suspects that there is a widening gap between what theologians and the clergy privately believe, and the official formularies of the bodies to which they belong. Yet nothing is done about it.

The other difficult question is that of the finality of Christ. Surely a Christian theologian has in some sense to claim that Christianity is the absolute truth and that other religions are only relatively true, or true only insofar as they approximate to Christianity? The Christian theologian says that there is no other name whereby men can be saved but that of Jesus. He will not concede that it is possible even in principle that Christianity might be superseded by another and better religion. He has to claim that the life and death of Jesus are the central episodes in the history of the universe.

However, the theologian also has to take account of other established principles which work against this. Wanting to distinguish between religious symbols and what they represent, he asserts the relativity of all religious symbols. He acknowledges the principle that outside the Church there is no salvation, yet he feels also obliged to admit that certain of the Sufi mystics attained to an authentic vision of God.

Clearly there is an acute difficulty here, which is felt in the theory of missions. Christians have been criticized for ruthlessly destroying beautiful pagan cultures. On the other hand, people have also criticized Christianity for not being rigorous enough in Latin America. People scoff at the missionaries who clothed Polynesians and shepherded them into Matins in Gothic Revival churches. But would those same people approve of voodoo? If a theologian contemplates the culture of an Amazonian tribesman or a Buddhist monk, he, as much as any other man, can regret that something beautiful is going to be destroyed,[1] and be perplexed about the question of the finality of Christ.

What a theologian is doing is this: he inherits a body of problems which will never be solved. He inherits a large body of theological principles of varying degrees of authority which cannot all be reconciled with each other. His attempt to make consistent sense of Christianity will never be wholly successful, rather as (in spite of all the philosophers who have at one time or another promised it) there will never be a final metaphysics. The theologian inherits traditional materials and methods, again very varied. He has his own human nature, his own experience of Christianity, and of the times he lives in. The task he undertakes is of enormous difficulty and complexity: but it is not foolish, even though it cannot be completed. Has Kaufmann noticed that some of the greatest theological enterprises were never completed, and that some of those who did complete their books went on to say that theology is by nature incompletable?

---

[1] I mean, by Western technological imperialism, a much more destructive force than ever missions were.

INDEX

ABBOTT, W. M., 57n., 73n.
ABÉLARD, PETER, 76, 102
ABRAHAM, 65, 111, 150
ADAM, 22, 24, 25f., 52f., 54, 65, 72, 99
AESCHYLUS, 65n.
ALLCHIN, A. M., 63n.
ALLPORT, G. W., 98n.
AMBROSE, ST., 73
ANAXAGORAS, 65n.
ANGELA OF FOLIGNO, 86n.
ANNAN, N., 23n., 89
ANSELM, ST., 18, 27n., 28, 151
AQUINAS, ST. THOMAS, 18, 48n., 52n., 55, 57, 62, 65, 66, 74, 81, 94, 148, 151
ARISTOTLE, 28, 48n., 51, 52n., 65n., 66, 67, 106f., 113
ARNOLD, MATTHEW, 14, 141f., 150
ATHANASIUS, 151
AUGUSTINE, ST., 17f., 19n., 20, 39, 45, 46, 48n., 54, 63f., 73, 80, 93, 139n.

BAILEY, D. S., 48n., 52n., 54n., 68n.
BAILLIE, J. B., 113n.
BARDOT, B., 60
BARRETT, C. K., 44
BARTH, K., 18, 68, 143, 146
"BEAUCHAMP, PHILIP", Ch. 7 *passim*
BEAUVOIR, S. DE, 48n., 53, 54n., 68
BENEDICT, ST., 36, 40, 43
BENTHAM, JEREMY, 28, 90, Ch. 7 *passim*
BERNARD, ST., 76
BESANT, ANNIE, 91
BEZZANT, J. S., 18
BLOUNT, CHARLES, 110
BOCCACCIO, 118
BONIFACE VIII, 72
BOSWELL, JAMES, 20
BOTTOMORE, T. B., 115n.
BOWLBY, JOHN, 60n.
BOWRING, JOHN, 125
BOYS SMITH, J. S., 110n.

BRADLAUGH, C., 91
BRANDON, S. G. F., 129n.
BRETALL, R., 29n.
BRIGHTMAN, E. S., 28n.
BROWN, CHRISTY, 96
BUBER, MARTIN, 149f.
BUDD, SUSAN, 22n., 98
BULTMANN, R., 146
BUTTERWORTH, G. W., 18n.

CAIRD, E., 23n.
CALVIN, CALVINISM, 18, 20, 21, 73, 74, 75, 135, 144, 150, 151
CAMPENHAUSEN, H. VON, 36, 39
CAMUS, A., 13n., 101n.
CARLILE, R., 125
CARTER, T. T., 63n.
CASTELLIO, 76, 102
CELSUS, 23
CHADWICK, H., 23n.
CHADWICK, W. O., 23n., 87n.
CHALMERS, A., 122n., 129n.
CHESTERTON, G. K., 84
CHILLINGWORTH, W., 80, 102
CHRISTOPHER, J. P., 17n., 18n.
CHRYSOSTOM, ST. JOHN, 76
CLAUDEL, P., 95
CLEMENT OF ALEXANDRIA, 102
COHEN, M. R., 133n.
COLERIDGE, S. T., 20f., 23n., 25f.
I Corinthians, 44n., 53n.
CORNFORD, F. M., 15n.
COTTON, J., 90
CREED, J. M., 110n.
CREIGHTON, M., 72n., 76, 82ff.

DANSETTE, A., 92n.
DANTE, 21, 81, 93, 148
DARWIN, CHARLES, 155
DAVID, 12
DEARNLEY, M., 78
DEISTS, 23, 110
DESCARTES, 68
DESMOULINS, MRS., 20n.

INDEX